Goodna Girls

A HISTORY OF CHILDREN IN A QUEENSLAND MENTAL ASYLUM

Aboriginal History Incorporated
Aboriginal History Inc. is a part of the Australian Centre for Indigenous History, Research School of Social Sciences, The Australian National University, and gratefully acknowledges the support of the School of History and the National Centre for Indigenous Studies, The Australian National University. Aboriginal History Inc. is administered by an Editorial Board which is responsible for all unsigned material. Views and opinions expressed by the author are not necessarily shared by Board members.

Contacting Aboriginal History
All correspondence should be addressed to the Editors, Aboriginal History Inc., ACIH, School of History, RSSS, 9 Fellows Road (Coombs Building), ANU, Acton, ACT, 2601, or aboriginalhistoryinc@gmail.com.

WARNING: Readers are notified that this publication includes personal references to child abuse and rape and may contain images of, and refer to, deceased persons.

Goodna Girls

A HISTORY OF CHILDREN IN A QUEENSLAND MENTAL ASYLUM

ADELE CHYNOWETH

PRESS

*In loving memory of other 'Goodna Girls' who also fought for justice—
Elaine, Heather, Joy, Judith, Cathy and Nell*

What man has nerve to do, man has not nerve to hear.
Harriet Beecher Stowe, *Uncle Tom's Cabin*, 1852

Published by ANU Press and Aboriginal History Inc.
The Australian National University
Acton ACT 2601, Australia
Email: anupress@anu.edu.au

Available to download for free at press.anu.edu.au

ISBN (print): 9781760463908
ISBN (online): 9781760463915

WorldCat (print): 1190868673
WorldCat (online): 1190867343

DOI: 10.22459/GG.2020

This title is published under a Creative Commons Attribution-NonCommercial-NoDerivatives 4.0 International (CC BY-NC-ND 4.0).

The full licence terms are available at
creativecommons.org/licenses/by-nc-nd/4.0/legalcode

Cover design and layout by ANU Press

Cover photograph: School photo of Jean/Erin, aged 7

This edition © 2020 ANU Press and Aboriginal History Inc.

Contents

Preface..xi
Acknowledgements...xv

Part 1: Historical Context
1. Marginalised Voices: The Quest for a Recognised History........3

Part 2: The Survivors
2. The Panther: Jean/Erin......................................27
3. One of the Most Persistent Bitches: Judy....................51
4. Wasted Days and Wasted Nights: Rose.........................77
5. Don't Shoot the Wounded: Tammy..............................85

Part 3: The Witnesses
6. Brewing Truth: The Priest..................................107
7. The Penny Dropped: The Psychiatrist........................115
8. I Had No Way of Processing What Was Going On: The Nurse...123

Part 4: Next Steps
9. Conclusion: What Followed and What May Yet Proceed........133
Glossary..141
Bibliography..151

Preface

The oral histories in this book include those of former female child patients who were sent to Goodna Asylum, later known as Wolston Park, an adult psychiatric facility in Queensland, Australia. This book grew out of a temporary touring exhibition that I curated, 'Inside: Life in Children's Homes and Institutions', which opened at the National Museum of Australia in November 2011. At the opening of that exhibition, I observed both celebration and resolution among former residents of children's institutions who, to this day, suffer the long-term effects of the abuse and neglect they experienced as children. However, there was little joy from the women who had been sent to Goodna. The exhibition did not assuage their feelings of resentment and lack of trust of those who inhabited professional positions. These women had unfinished business. At the launch of the exhibition, they turned to me and asked: 'Are you going to help us get justice?'

Within the wider history of institutionalised 'care' in Australia, I knew that the history of children in Wolston Park was marginalised and deserving of further attention. The 1998 Commission of Inquiry into the Abuse of Children in Queensland Institutions, known as the 'Forde Inquiry', had excluded adult psychiatric facilities from its terms of reference and so these former child inmates were ineligible for the subsequent financial redress scheme. On 24 March 2010, the Queensland Government had apologised to former children under state care who had been placed in adult mental hospitals, and had stated its intention to hold reconciliation talks with survivors. The framed apology document was subsequently lost and the government did not follow through with the reconciliation talks as promised. Even though my temporary position at the National Museum of Australia had concluded, I decided to do what I could—with my own personal resources, and within the bounds of my qualifications and area of professional expertise, as well as academic research ethics—to draw public attention to the experiences of this group of women survivors. These oral histories are a mere sample of a cohort of former Goodna child patients who had been waiting for recognition of their childhood experiences and a just resolution. The research for this book was thus part of a wider campaign to seek justice for former state wards of adult psychiatric facilities.

The women were well-organised and highly articulate, but those in power continually refused to pay meaningful attention and follow-up of their legitimate and well-founded pleas. I wanted the Queensland Government to know that others, apart from these courageous survivors, were watching, and that their reasonable pleas mattered. I knew that the need for mediation by someone occupying a professional job was a form of elitism. They should have been acknowledged in their own right by those in power, as should their experiences of their own living history. The need for professional mediation and/or the clout from a prestigious organisation was a failure of democracy, in my view. Nevertheless, having been asked to assist, I chose to find out how I could shove my proverbial foot in a parliamentary door, knowing full well that I would likely be injured, discredited and scapegoated. The alternative—doing nothing—was not an option: the prospect of the distress I knew I would feel if I turned my back on these women seemed far worse. Further, in addition to writing and talking *about* a topic, I discovered the imperative to *do* something *with others*.

I applied to become an honorary fellow at The Australian National University (ANU) so that I could have access to research and ethical resources. In supporting my application, and through its ongoing professional disinterested role, ANU has become part of the living history that informs this book—a keen reminder of the need for independent universities. In 2012, the university's strategic communications team played a critical role in co-writing and distributing a media release about my research.[1] Subsequently, Fairfax Press printed a series of newspaper articles, written by Amy Remeikis, about the plight of Wolston Park survivors.[2] On 6 March 2013, the Queensland Government repeated the apology it had made in 2010, but, yet again, it did not schedule reconciliation talks with survivors.

---

1   'Remembering Forgotten Australians', 13 August 2012, ANU College of Arts and Social Sciences, accessed 5 October 2019, cass.anu.edu.au/news/remembering-forgotten-australians.
2   See, for example, Amy Remeikis, 'Come Clean on Chambers of Horrors, Sufferers Plead', 19 August 2012, *The Sydney Morning Herald*, accessed 5 October 2019, www.smh.com.au/national/come-clean-on-chambers-of-horrors-sufferers-plead-20120818-24fqx.html.

PREFACE

In 2013, a Royal Commission into Institutional Responses to Child Sexual Abuse was established by the Australian Government. I was asked to attend a private hearing on 24 April 2015 at which I spoke, tabled my research, and emphasised the importance of a public case study, as part of the commission, concerning the abuse of children in adult psychiatric facilities. The commission's refusal to act on this prompted me to write, in consultation with survivors, an opinion piece that was published online in 2016.[3] Queensland's acting mental health commissioner took notice, contacting me a few days later[4] and subsequently liaising with others within the Queensland Government. This seemed like a positive development, but there was no way to know whether the government would follow through with restorative justice. In February 2017, the Queensland Department of Health announced a formal reconciliation process for those who, 'as children, were in the care of the State and inappropriately placed in Queensland adult mental health facilities'.[5]

This was definite progress. Yet, no details concerning when the process would commence and whether or not it would result in reparation for survivors was released. Some of the women and I had been talking to journalist Matthew Condon in the hope that he might write a newspaper article informed by the voices of survivors. Condon's 5,000-word feature appeared in the *Courier Mail* on 11 March 2017.[6] The title captured the struggle: 'House of Horrors—Survivors Fight for Justice after Enduring Unspeakable Abuse as Young Girls in a Brisbane Asylum'. Matthew Condon had joined the ranks of a small number of journalists—namely Ken Blanch, Steve Austin and Amy Remeikis—who understood the need to draw public attention to the women's quest for much needed recompense. Five days after Condon's article was published, Queensland's Minister for Health Cameron Dick spoke on radio about his commitment to an authentic reconciliation process, which, he assured, would include financial reparation.[7] In October 2017, each of the survivors who had participated in the reconciliation process received letters from the

---

[3] Chynoweth, 'Who Is Protected'.
[4] Email to author, 27 March 2016.
[5] Queensland Government, *Fact Sheet 1*, 1.
[6] Matthew Condon, 'House of Horrors—Survivors Fight for Justice after Enduring Unspeakable Abuse as Young Girls in a Brisbane Asylum', *The Courier Mail*, 11 March 2017.
[7] This occurred on ABC Radio, Brisbane, 16 March 2017. The reporter was Steve Austin.

Queensland Government that detailed a list of reparations, including ex gratia payments. It had been almost six years since the opening of the 'Inside' exhibition and the call for justice.

The research that informed our campaign is now made public in these pages. Through *Goodna Girls*, I hope for public acknowledgement of this living history so that it is never repeated. There are implications here for current child protection policies and for an inclusive public history. To those who hold power in the fields of law and government; who advise on policies; who analyse material culture; who keep, write and exhibit narratives; who are paid to care; who teach—I commend the narratives in this book as a baton for your steadfast hold and resolute journey along the path of justice.

Adele Chynoweth
20 August 2020

Acknowledgements

Thank you to the ANU Press Publication Subisdy Fund, Paul Ashton, Joanna Besley, Frank Bongiorno, Clare Campbell, Samuel Clark, Matthew Condon, Helen Glazebrook, Evana Ho, Catriona Jackson, Hayley Jenkins, Lorena Kanellopoulos, Rani Kerin, Jill Julius Matthews, Ann McGrath, John Murray, Kath McFarlane, Maria Nugent, Martyn Pearce, Katharine Pierce, Teresa Prowse, Amy Remeikis, Vanessa Rouse, Laurajane Smith, Carolyn Strange, Emily Tinker, Christine Waite, Lucy Wedlock, Tikka Wilson and Angela Woollacott.

To the following members of the Federation of International Human Rights Museums who supported my conference presentation on this subject in 2017 at the Museo Internacional para la Democracia in Rosario, Argentina: David Fleming, Françoise McClafferty, Susana Meden, Jane Smith and Guillermo Whpei.

To those whose lives are recounted here, I extend my profound gratitude for your courage and trust and, indeed, for all that you have taught me, including the strength in camaraderie. My life has been forever changed. I will never forget.

PART 1: HISTORICAL CONTEXT

1
Marginalised Voices: The Quest for a Recognised History

Goodna Girls is a firsthand history of the consequences of a policy that resulted in children being incarcerated in an adult psychiatric hospital. What follows is a collection of oral histories of four former child inmates (Jean/Erin, Judy, Rose and Tammy) and three staff (the priest, the psychiatrist and the nurse) from Wolston Park Hospital, Queensland's oldest and largest mental health facility. Wolston Park was founded in 1865 as Woogaroo Lunatic Asylum. It changed its name to Goodna Asylum (later Hospital) for the Insane in 1880 and is now known as The Park Centre for Mental Health. As Mark Finnane and Joanna Besley note, each name change reflected an 'aspiration to escape the stigma associated with an institution for "the insane"'.[1] Before Woogaroo was established, male and female 'lunatics' had been lodged at the Brisbane Gaol. The name 'Woogaroo', which means 'to step over a person lying down', was derived from an Aboriginal name for the land on which the asylum was built.[2] Between 1867 and 1915, five parliamentary inquiries and royal commissions were held into the asylum's management and accommodation.[3] Over 50,000 patients were admitted there between 1865 and the mid-1980s.[4]

---

1 Besley and Finnane, 'Remembering Goodna', 117.
2 Finnane, 'Wolston Park Hospital', 39.
3 Finnane, 'Wolston Park Hospital', 43.
4 Finnane, 'Wolston Park Hospital', 52.

There is no certainty about the number of child patients admitted to Goodna. In March 2017, Queensland's Minister for Health, Cameron Dick, stated that approximately 50–60 children had been sent to Goodna, but he did not provide any details about the years of their admission or the source of his figures.[5] The women interviewed for this book have letters, written at the time of their admission, from Queensland's departments of Health and Children's Services. However, these departments claim that they 'do not have any data' for 'children under the age of 18 admitted to the Park Centre for Mental Health'.[6] The Department of Health did not begin to collect patient data for psychiatric hospitals until the 1995/96 financial year.[7] Finnane and Besley claim that Wolston Park has an archive of medical records that 'are not open to the public and access by researchers is strictly vetted'.[8]

Child 'Protection'

Goodna Girls is part of a wider history of institutionalised welfare policies and practices that emerged during the nineteenth century in the wake of the Industrial Revolution, which saw masses of people relocate to areas that grew into large cities. The growth of a pauper class prompted the formation of charitable organisations[9] and new practices of state monitoring and attempts to control individuals and communities through social welfare agencies.[10] For vulnerable children, one of the outcomes of this conflation of scrutiny and social work was their institutionalisation—a practice referred to as 'penal welfarism'. Kerry Carrington defines penal welfarism as 'the punishment of children for non-criminal conduct under status or welfare offences, such as being uncontrollable or exposed to moral danger'.[11]

Penal welfarism in Australia dates back to the earliest times of European colonisation. Fifteen per cent of all convicts transported to Australia between 1788 and 1868 were aged 18 or younger.[12] During the nineteenth

---

5   This occurred on ABC Radio, Brisbane, 16 March 2017. The reporter was Steve Austin.
6   Child Safety After Hours, Brisbane Region, email to author, 3 May 2016.
7   Queensland Department of Health, email to author, 18 April 2016.
8   Besley and Finnane, 'Remembering Goodna', 120.
9   Ferguson, *Protecting Children in Time*, 27–29.
10   Ferguson, *Protecting Children in Time*, 17.
11   Carrington, *Offending Youth*, 9.
12   Kociumbas, *Australian Childhood*, 21.

century, industrial schools and reformatories, which were often run like prisons, were established around the country. In 1871, in Queensland, abandoned or criminal boys were housed on the *Proserpine*, a hulk anchored in the Brisbane River, near Lytton,[13] echoing the British prison hulks of the late eighteenth century. Penal welfarism continued into the twentieth century, with over 900 orphanages, homes and other residential facilities for children operating in Australia.[14]

For decades, child protection policies have been conflated with institutionalised punishment and treatments of mental illness. For example, alcohol abuse was linked with delinquency in Queensland's *Inebriates Institutions Act 1896*, which permitted substance abusers, including young people, to be placed in psychiatric facilities.[15] During the 1950s in Brisbane, girls from the industrial schools—Sisters of Mercy's Holy Cross Home; Mt Maria Re-Education Centre, Mitchelton, run by the Sisters of the Good Shepherd; and the Salvation Army's Kalimna Vocational Centre—could be sent to psychiatric hospitals if they were deemed disruptive. Dedicated psychiatric facilities for children were established in Queensland in the 1960s. Karrala House, for girls, was opened in 1963 within the Ipswich Mental Hospital and was administered by Queensland's State Children Department. Wilson Youth Hospital had been established for boys (up to the age of 14) in 1961, with a section for girls opening in 1971. What prompted this development?

Fear of 'Delinquents'

The emergence of youth cultures after World War II (WWII) provoked moral panic around a perceived epidemic of juvenile delinquency.[16] The Australian 'bodgies and widgies' of the 1950s were one of the targets of this dread, exemplified by A. E. Manning's book *The Bodgie: A Study in Psychological Abnormality* (1959), which cast this cohort as juvenile delinquents in need of psychiatric treatment.[17] The Queensland police formed a 'Bodgie Squad' in the Brisbane Police District.[18] At the same time, the medical response to young people from the working and poverty classes was formalised in government policy.

---

13   Stathis, 'An Historical Account', 588.
14   Find & Connect, accessed 14 February 2020, www.findandconnect.gov.au/.
15   Stathis, 'An Historical Account', 590.
16   Bessant, 'Described, Measured and Labelled', 8; Moore, 'Bodgies, Widgies and Moral Panic'.
17   Stratton, 'Bodgies and Widgies', 11–12.
18   Queensland Government, *Report of the Committee on Youth Problems*, 18.

In 1957, Queensland Premier (Sir) Frank Nicklin constituted a Committee on Youth Problems, chaired by Police Minister Alexander Tattenhall Dewar. Tasked with addressing youth problems, such as neglected children and criminal delinquents, the committee recommended the establishment of Child Guidance Clinics led by a psychiatrist. Referrals could be made by order of a judge or magistrate in a specific Juvenile Court Clinic that would be instituted for the purpose.[19] The committee also recommended that police be 'authorised to request the parents of children found to be committing anti-social acts to direct such children to the Children's Court Clinic'.[20]

In 1961, a Committee on Child Welfare Legislation was appointed by the Minister for Health and Home Affairs. Chaired by Minister Dewar, the committee, which comprised members of the departments of Justice, Health and Home Affairs and the director of the State Children Department, observed the lack of research linking delinquency and mental illness. Yet, although there were 'no accurate figures available for the incidence of delinquency and its relationship to psychiatric abnormality', the committee reported that 'the Senior Medical Director of the Welfare and Guidance Service has formed the *opinion* that the incidence of personality disorder and psychiatric abnormality amongst delinquent youth in this State is high'.[21]

This opinion informed the establishment of the Wilson Youth Hospital in 1961 for the 'assessment, remand and treatment' of teenage boys and also Karrala House in 1963 for 'the older and more recalcitrant type of girl'.[22] The Committee on Child Welfare Legislation's report discussed different categories of 'care' in accordance with Queensland's *State Children Act 1911* and *Children's Court Act 1907*, and recommended that 'voluntary admission to care', then limited to the age of 14, be raised to 18.[23] However, according to the State Children Act, girls could legally be in the protective care of the state, even if not institutionalised, until they were 21.

---

19   Queensland Government, *Report of the Committee on Youth Problems*, 8–9.
20   Queensland Government, *Report of the Committee on Youth Problems*, 17.
21   Queensland Government, *Report of the Committee on Child Welfare*, 7 (emphasis added).
22   Queensland Government, *Report of the Committee on Child Welfare*, 22.
23   Queensland Government, *Report of the Committee on Child Welfare*, 3.

That this form of institutionalisation endured beyond the 'bodgie and widgie' era may be explained by the broader notion of the 'deviant':

> Those particularly susceptible to being labelled 'deviant' are those whose deviance is public and visible. This means that particular groups of people with high levels of public visibility, such as Indigenous people, young people in rural communities, homeless youth, visible ethnic minorities, young people who hang out in public spaces or shopping malls tend to become the locus of adverse public and police attention and labelled as deviant.[24]

The decisions of the Committee on Child Welfare Legislation in the 1960s were also set against a wider, international backdrop of social engineering informed by eugenics and euthenics. Prior to WWII, when it became associated with Nazi Germany, eugenics had been a popular movement in most Western countries, including Australia.[25] The theory of eugenics was first developed in England, during the Victorian era, by Francis Galton, a cousin of Charles Darwin. Galton believed that heredity had more influence on individual characteristics than environment. He advocated for the collection and publication of eugenics data and the discouragement of procreation among those considered unfit. In eugenic terms, he favoured the wealthy.[26] English eugenicist Caleb Saleeby supported positive and negative eugenics:

> Negative eugenics relates to the problem of preventing the mental and physical defectives of society from perpetuating their defects through propagation. Positive eugenics relates to the problem of improving the mass of mankind by the selection of the superior in the process of reproduction.[27]

Even though discredited, eugenic philosophy informed discourses on the most vulnerable in society, including adolescents.[28]

---

24   Carrington, *Offending Youth*, 46.
25   Wilson, *Prevention is Better than Cure*, 1.
26   Semmel, 'Karl Pearson: Socialist and Darwinist', 118–19.
27   Ward, 'Eugenics, Euthenics, and Eudemics', 738.
28   Wilson, *Prevention is Better than Cure*, 174.

By contrast, euthenics is the theory that environmental factors can temper hereditary predispositions.[29] Historian Stephen Garton maintains that, in Australia, social problems were perceived to be the result of both hereditary and environmental factors, which influenced the 'mental hygiene' movement. This interplay, Garton reasons, can be understood via the Foucauldian concept of 'bio-politics', which:

> United a broad cross section of professional middle-class opinion … [and] eventually had a significant impact on those subjected to the new mental hygiene gaze, through the psychologists, teachers, social workers and psychiatrists who have come to be employed in many government departments and private welfare organisations since the 1930s.[30]

The preoccupation with 'mental hygiene' and social problems is reflected in a statement in 1956 by Robert Heffron, New South Wales Deputy Premier and Minister for Education, who surmised that neglected children were virulent: 'Deprived children, whether in their own homes or out of them, are a source of social infection as real and serious as are carriers of diphtheria and typhoid.'[31] American social theorist Erving Goffman coined the term 'total institution' to describe places of residence where people were isolated from wider society, such as orphanages, mental asylums and detention centres. These total institutions were designed, at least in part, to protect 'the wider population from contamination'.[32] If neglected children were deemed contagious, then their institutionalisation was used as a form of social protection for the masses.

Lack of Education

The narratives within *Goodna Girls* demonstrate how the talents of marginalised children may be overlooked. Jean/Erin recalls how she was bored at school because she learned content very quickly. Tammy was diagnosed with savant syndrome, but neither girl's talent was nurtured by formal education. This observation remains relevant for current education policy. A recent Victorian Government inquiry into the

---

29 Ward, 'Eugenics, Euthenics, and Eudemics', 748; Cole, 'Stolen Babies', 148.
30 Garton, 'Sound Minds', 181.
31 Penglase, *Orphans of the Living*, 241.
32 Penglase, *Orphans of the Living*, 103–04.

education of gifted and talented students notes that gifted children come from all backgrounds and that some students are at risk of not having their gifts identified:

> Students at particular risk of having their abilities overlooked are those from backgrounds of educational disadvantage such as low socioeconomic, Indigenous or culturally and linguistically diverse backgrounds, as well as students who live in rural and regional areas and students with disabilities.[33]

Tammy, who was also diagnosed as autistic, recounts the physical abuse she encountered in primary school. Reports of the abuse of children with disabilities in schools continue to be heard today, including the use of unsupervised restraints for children diagnosed with autism.[34] In June 2017, One Nation senator Pauline Hanson suggested in parliament that children with autism should be educated in a 'special classroom'.[35] Although Hanson's comments were not based on research, they still provoked debate, including responses from journalists such as Guy Rundle who argued that the range of behaviours of children in a post-industrial society need to be considered, and that a more modular process of teaching, beyond the 'one-size-fits-all classroom', is called for.[36] Tammy's testimony contributes to such debates. In terms of democratic decision-making, it highlights the implications of excluding the voices of those to whom the benefits or disadvantages of government policies may flow.

Archival Records

The narratives in this book demonstrate the effects on survivors of the personal records that were kept by the state and by institutions. According to Jean/Erin, her incarceration at Boggo Road Gaol as an adult was enabled by a prosecuting lawyer who erroneously concluded that her

---

33   Education and Training Committee, *Inquiry*, xxiv.
34   Louise Milligan, 'School Investigated after Claims Boy with Autism Locked in "Cage"', *ABC News*, 16 August 2016, accessed 20 September 2019, www.abc.net.au/news/2016-08-16/school-investigated-after-claims-boy-with-autism/7749726.
35   Jane Norman and Eliza Borrello, 'Pauline Hanson under Fire for "Bigoted" Call to Remove Children with Disabilities from Mainstream Classrooms', 22 June 2017, *ABC News*, accessed 29 September 2019, www.abc.net.au/news/2017-06-21/pauline-hanson-under-fire-repulsive-bigoted-comments-autism/8640328.
36   Guy Rundle, 'Hanson's Autistic Kids Comments Reveal a Truth No One Wants to Talk About', 23 June 2017, *Crikey*, accessed 29 September 2019, www.crikey.com.au/2017/06/23/hansons-autistic-kids-comments-reveal-a-truth-no-one-wants-to-talk-about/.

institutional files were evidence of a juvenile criminal record. Similarly, Tammy recounts how her personal files render her vulnerable to being misunderstood when accessed by health professionals today.

The records of those who were institutionalised as children have the 'capacity to revive past suffering' and 'disrupt an individual's sense of self'.[37] Not only did many institutionalised children endure violent abuse, but also their lives were the subject of relentless and excessive scrutiny by those in positions of power. Record keeping was, and remains, a central mechanism in this constant and invasive monitoring of children in out-of-home care. The potential for the content of these files to be deemed 'objective' by those who access them disavows the personal and moral judgements that inform their creation. Sometimes, survivors try to access these records to piece together their histories and provide evidence of their time in 'care'. Jacqueline Z. Wilson and Frank Golding advocate for the reform of file-keeping methods to enable survivors to actively participate in the creation of their own files.[38]

Livia Iacovino notes the way in which record keeping has enabled the surveillance of Indigenous communities. Human rights may be compromised when the records of Aboriginal and Torres Strait Islander peoples are held by non-Indigenous organisations. Iacovino proposes a 'participant model' of archival reform, which may include Indigenous communities having full ownership rights[39] and formal acknowledgement of 'multiple record creators'.[40] As former Aboriginal and Torres Strait Islander Social Justice Commissioner Mick Gooda noted:

> It is the role of government and others, including archivists and recordkeepers, to position themselves to enable Aboriginal and Torres Strait Islanders to move from passive and powerless subjects to active participatory agents. I hope my insights assist in pushing towards an archive and recordkeeping system that facilitates the active participation of Aboriginal and Torres Strait Island peoples.[41]

A participatory methodology has implications for historical archives as well as current and future record keeping. A recent Australian Research Council–funded project by researchers from Monash and Federation

---

37   Wilson and Golding, 'Latent Scrutiny', 93.
38   Wilson and Golding, 'Latent Scrutiny', 95, 97, 99, 107.
39   Iacovino, 'Rethinking', 362–63.
40   Iacovino, 'Rethinking', 367.
41   McKemmish et al., 'Decolonizing Recordkeeping'.

universities, 'Rights in Records by Design', emphasises the views of those who have experienced out-of-home care. Another project, 'Indigenous Archiving and Cultural Safety', has been undertaken by Indigenous researcher Kirsten Thorpe and uses community-based participation approaches, including 'yarning', to deconstruct colonial power relationships and associated structural barriers.[42] Iacovino stresses the need to acknowledge 'oral memory' as an important source of Indigenous knowledge.[43] The memories shared in *Goodna Girls* exemplify the grievous consequences of colonising surveillance facilitated by discriminatory archival practices. Given that Aboriginal and Torres Strait Islander children comprised 36.9 per cent of children in out-of-home care on 30 June 2017,[44] an ethical, participatory record-keeping policy and practice is a current imperative.

Staff Witnesses

This book includes the narratives of three former staff members at Goodna. These provide insight into the systemic barriers staff faced in attempting to support their patients. The priest, a former chaplain at Wilson Youth Hospital, told his story at a time when public criticism of the Catholic Church was rife.[45] Alive to such criticism, he describes the struggle to realise a democratic church. He refers to the importance of Vatican II, established in 1959, which aimed to realise the direction of Pope John XXIII to 'usher the church into modernity'. Among other changes, this resulted in the introduction of folk music and guitars in the Catholic mass.[46] However, it would be naive to assume that the abuse of children within the church was perpetrated solely by autocratic clergy members with a pre-Vatican II sensibility: 'guitar-playing' priests have also been accused of sexual abuse.[47]

---

42 McKemmish et al., 'Decolonizing Recordkeeping'.
43 Iacovino, 'Rethinking', 356.
44 Australian Government, Australian Institute of Family Studies, 'Children in Care', September 2018, accessed 1 October 2019, aifs.gov.au/cfca/publications/children-care#targetText=The%20 remaining%206.7%25%20of%20children,for%20between%201%E2%80%932%20years.
45 Royal Commission into Institutional Responses to Child Sexual Abuse, *Final Report*.
46 Oppenheimer, 'Folk Music in the Catholic Mass', 103–04.
47 Padraig Collins, 'Irish Priests Keep Working Despite Abuse Allegations', 18 May 2010, *The Irish Times*, accessed 26 September 2019, www.irishtimes.com/news/irish-priests-kept-working-despite-abuse-allegations-1.666495.

The priest's account draws attention to a significant international movement in the Catholic Church—the paradigm of liberation theology, attributed to the Peruvian Dominican priest Gustavo Gutiérrez. Liberation theology has been simplistically labelled as a mixture of Christianity and Marxism. It is perhaps more apt to describe it as a way of positioning Christianity from the perspective of the poor.[48] The priest explains how his work with homeless youth was influenced by his study of liberation theology. This description illustrates the lack of targeted and relevant social services for youth at risk at a time when state government responses tended to be characterised by punitive welfarism. The priest, in his role at Wilson Youth Hospital, witnessed the transition of some child inmates to Wolston Park Hospital, prompting him to visit them after their relocation.

In addition to the priest's account, *Goodna Girls* includes oral histories of a psychiatrist and a student nurse who worked at Wolston Park Hospital. Both witnessed violence against patients at the hands of other staff and encountered obstacles in seeking justice for these crimes. The psychiatrist reported witnessing a nurse using force to administer medicine to a teenage patient and later gave evidence in court. However, the nurse was not convicted. When the student nurse reported seeing a nurse raping a patient, the tyres on her car were slashed. In the interests of her safety, she was transferred from the ward. But was the perpetrator brought to justice? Transferring witnesses and offenders does not ensure the safety of vulnerable people.

In his narrative, the psychiatrist notes that mental health facilities may be used inappropriately to detain those who are deemed difficult to control. However, he states that 'self-harm and aggression don't always correlate with the person having a mental illness'. The psychiatrist also speaks to what he understands as his former, middle-class, judgemental approach to child protection. Such personal insight may be explained with reference to the theory of cultural relativism, in 'that rights (and other social practices, values, and moral rules) are culturally determined'.[49] This understanding or position is not unique to the psychiatrist. As Clark observes:

---

48 Berryman, *Liberation Theology*, 4.
49 Donnelly, 'Cultural Relativism', 401.

> Social workers are intensely sensitive to charges of being middle class and judgemental, and vigorously pursue approaches which are regarded as non-directive and non-judgmental, and avoid imposing any set of values—and particularly one's own set—on the client.[50]

Beyond middle-class judgementalism, critical insights might come from querying the efficacy of child protection services.

'Care-Criminalisation'[51]

A unifying discursive thread runs through the oral histories in *Goodna Girls*: the children who were deemed to be 'at risk' in domestic settings, or in other settings such as school, were not better served in government-sanctioned, out-of-home 'care' settings. This observation is still relevant today, yet it seems that the lessons have not been learned.

In 2016, the Victorian Government Department of Health and Human Services engaged global finance company KPMG and the Australian Childhood Foundation (ACF) to address the problem of children suffering from trauma in out-of-home care. The subsequent report recommended the development of a set of options for a 'contained therapeutic and treatment care service' (CTTCS) for vulnerable children in Victoria. Children as young as eight years old who had experienced trauma and had previously been subject to secure welfare services would be eligible for CTTCS via a court order. The KPMG and ACF report also proposed that the staffing of CTTCS's should include mental health specialists.[52] While the Victorian Government rejected the recommendations within the report, it is alarming that recognisable parallels with the historical proposals of the Queensland Government's committees on Child Welfare Legislation (1963) and Youth Problems (1959) could be conceived by policymakers today.[53] Rather than place vulnerable children who suffer from trauma in psychiatric lock-up facilities, Lesley McAra and Susan McVie conclude that 'justice for children and young people cannot

---

50 Clark, 'Child Protection', 20.
51 A term coined by Kath McFarlane in her article, 'Care-Criminalisation'.
52 KPMG and Australian Childhood Foundation, 'A Proposed Contained Therapeutic Treatment', 6.
53 Dan Oakes, 'Vic Government Rejects Recommendations to Set up Facility Forcing Children into Treatment', *ABC Radio*, 14 February 2017, accessed 29 September 2019, www.abc.net.au/radio/programs/pm/vic-government-rejects-recommendations-to-set-up/8270472.

be delivered unless their broader needs are addressed in ways that are not stigmatising and criminalising'.[54] They note the importance of 'understanding the cumulative impact of agency intervention over many years (which is deleterious in some cases)'.[55] Had KPMG and the ACF consulted adults who had experienced out-of-home care as children, would their recommendations have differed?

The narratives in *Goodna Girls* demonstrate a clear link between the child protection system and homelessness. A recent Australian survey found that 63 per cent of homeless youth respondents had been placed in some form of out-of-home care by their eighteenth birthday.[56] This book also illustrates a connection between out-of-home care and the criminal justice system. Jean/Erin was placed in Boggo Road Gaol as an adult. Judy relates her sister Beverley's pathway from abuse at Parramatta Girls' Home to prostitution to incarceration in Long Bay Gaol.

A study of New South Wales prison populations found that 30 per cent of respondents had lived in out-of-home care before the age of 16.[57] Other studies, conducted in 2009 and 2014, found that the proportion of children from out-of-home care ranged from 19 to 34 per cent, respectively.[58] The Australian Institute of Criminology has noted the over-representation of individuals in the criminal justice system who, as children, were subject to child protection, finding that they are 'at least nine times more likely than other young people to offend and come under the supervision of youth justice services'.[59] These findings are echoed internationally. The Howard League for Prison Reform in the United Kingdom found that 'children aged 16 and 17 living in children's homes are at least 15 times more likely to be criminalised than other children of the same age'.[60] Research conducted in Canada in 2009 found that children in out-of-home care were 'eight times more likely to appear before a criminal court than children in the general population'.[61]

---

54 McAra and McVie, 'Delivering Justice', 3.
55 McAra and McVie, 'Delivering Justice', 9.
56 MacKenzie et al., 'The Cost of Youth Homelessness'.
57 Cited in McFarlane, 'Care-Criminalisation', 414–15.
58 McFarlane, 'Care-Criminalisation', 413.
59 Cited in Baidawi and Sheehan, 'Crossover Kids'.
60 Howard League for Penal Reform, *Ending the Criminalisation*.
61 McFarlane, 'Care-Criminalisation', 413–14.

A 2019 report by the Queensland Productivity Commission identified risk factors for contact with the criminal justice system. In early childhood, these include 'parental absence', 'lack of a stable home environment', 'abuse or trauma' and 'removal from home'.[62] The report cited the findings of the Griffith University Criminology Institute, which found that 'offenders are more likely to have contact with child protection or mental health services': 52 per cent of people who had a recorded history of childhood maltreatment and 52 per cent of people with a mental illness hospitalisation had offended.[63] Australian criminal justice scholar Kath McFarlane terms this 'care-criminalisation' and notes that the institutions charged with the care of children facilitate this pathway to prison through punitive responses to children's behavioural concerns, which are often trauma related. This punitive approach is evident in the narratives in *Goodna Girls*. These oral histories, together with current research concerning child protection, build a strong case for non-punitive, trauma-informed responses to vulnerable children.

Escape from Goodna

At different times, Jean/Erin, Rosie and Judy all broke out of Wolston Park Hospital only to be arrested and returned to the site of their abuse and neglect. Jean/Erin and Rosie escaped a second time and lived the rest of their teenage years on the run to avoid further remand. Judy remained at Wolston Park following her return until she was legally eligible to be discharged. Tammy escaped with the assistance of an empathetic nurse and Lady Phyllis Cilento, a medical practitioner and prominent medical journalist who has been the subject of strong criticism in recent years. Tammy casts Cilento as a hero. Yet, in 2018, the Queensland Government was criticised for naming one of its Brisbane hospitals after her. Approximately 900 hospital staff signed a petition in protest against the use of Cilento's name due to her racist and homophobic views, evident in the columns she wrote in newspapers and magazines.[64] Cilento was well known for supporting the administering of high vitamin dosages to children, and Tammy recalls that she gave her vitamins after her escape from Wolston Park.

---

62 Queensland Productivity Commission, *Inquiry into Imprisonment*.
63 Queensland Productivity Commission, *Inquiry into Imprisonment*.
64 Ben Smee, 'Staff Call for Hospital Renaming over Lady Cilento's Racist and Homophobic Views', *The Guardian*, 28 August 2018, accessed 10 September 2019, www.theguardian.com/australia-news/2018/aug/28/staff-call-for-hospital-renaming-over-lady-cilentos-racist-and-homophobic-views.

Cilento helped Tammy escape, but what did she do for other child inmates at Wolston Park? Tammy's narrative sheds light on the role of accidental heroes in testimonies of trauma—random elements of hope in an otherwise unyielding system. Her narrative evokes the invisible accounts of children in the wards who were left behind. What was their fate? Further research is required to examine the number of children who were admitted to Wolston Park, whether or not they were discharged, and what happened to them.

The Quest for Justice

On 29 September 1996, Brisbane newspaper the *Sunday Mail* published an article entitled 'Goodna's Secret Wards' based on journalist Ken Blanch's interviews with former child inmates who were sent to Ward 8 of Wolston Park Hospital.[65] Blanch mentioned that Judith Veness (since deceased), a former child inmate of Wolston Park, was inviting others to contact her in the hope of forming a support group to seek compensation from the Queensland Government. Jean/Erin describes how she met Judith and others to collectively lobby for justice. She recalls how this group of Goodna survivors sought legal support, and that her case was put forward in the Supreme Court of Brisbane as a test case. However, the State of Queensland claimed, successfully, that the case was barred by the *Limitation of Actions Act 1974*, which stated that legal actions for personal injury must be commenced within three years from the date of the injury.

In September 2015, the Royal Commission into Institutional Responses to Child Sexual Abuse recommended the removal of any limitation period 'as soon as possible'.[66] In May 2016, the Queensland Government announced that it would conduct community consultations as part of statutory reforms. In November that year, the Queensland Government passed the Limitation of Actions (Institutional Child Sexual Abuse) and Other Legislation Amendment Bill 2016, which removed the limitation periods for civil litigation for survivors of child sexual abuse.[67] Even more recently, in October 2019, the Queensland Government passed the *Civil Liability and Other Legislation Amendment Act 2019,* which expanded the definition of abuse to include physical and psychological abuse.

---

65   Ken Blanch, 'Goodna's Secret Wards', *The Sunday Mail* (Brisbane), 29 September 1996, Scope, 61.
66   Royal Commission into Institutional Responses to Child Sexual Abuse, *Redress*, 52.
67   Queensland Government, *Limitations of Actions*.

Government Inquiries into Institutionalised Child Abuse

The Forde Inquiry

From 1852 to 2013 there have been 83 inquiries into the institutionalisation of children in Australia.[68] Since the 1990s, nine countries have initiated inquiries into institutionalised child abuse following extensive and enduring campaigning from those who have experienced institutionalised 'care' as children.[69] In 1998, as a result of over 10 years of activism from survivor groups, Queensland's Minister for Families, Youth and Community Care Anna Bligh established a Commission of Inquiry into Abuse of Children in Queensland Institutions, known as the 'Forde Inquiry'. One of the outcomes of the Forde Inquiry was the establishment of a redress scheme. The government's acknowledgement of its responsibility for systemic harm led to the provision of financial redress in the form of ex gratia payments.[70] Redress aims to protect survivors from the confronting process of cross-examination in court. However, redress also protects the government that implemented neglectful child protective systems from being cast in court as the defendant (of such abuse) in the face of survivors. The terms of reference of the Forde Inquiry were limited to those institutions that pertained to the *State Children Act 1911*, the *Children's Services Act 1965* or the *Juvenile Justice Act 1992*.[71] Wolston Park Hospital operated under the *Mental Health Act 1962*.[72] Therefore, those state wards who were transferred there as children were prevented from testifying at the Forde Inquiry about their experiences of being institutionalised in an adult mental health facility and, in turn, were ineligible for ex gratia payments as part of the redress scheme that operated from 2007 to 2010.[73]

---

68 Swain, *History of Australian*.
69 Sköld, 'Historical Abuse', 6.
70 Winter, 'Australia's Ex Gratia Redress', 49.
71 Queensland Government, *Report of the Commission of Inquiry into Abuse*, 3.
72 Finnane, 'Wolston Park Hospital', 41.
73 These survivors, however, were eligible for a redress payment for abuse suffered in children's institutions prior to being sent to Wolston Park. Nevertheless, it cannot be assumed that such payments recompensed those specific physical, emotional and social consequences of internment at Wolston Park.

The Forde Inquiry and the Not-For-Profit Sector

Project Esther began in Brisbane in 1994 to address violence in Christian communities. Renamed the 'Esther Centre' in 1998, it helped victims of institutionalised child abuse prepare submissions to the Forde Inquiry. The centre was renamed 'Lotus Place' in 2006. It continues to provide support for those who have experienced institutionalised abuse.[74] Staff at Lotus Place helped Jean/Erin discover her Aboriginal identity. Judy, in her narrative, mentions that Lotus Place staff were present during a public meeting about the Forde Inquiry. Lotus Place also hosts the Historical Abuse Network (HAN), an advocacy group of survivors of institutionalised abuse, formed in 2000.[75] Despite, or perhaps because of, episodic interactions between the women in this book and Lotus Place staff, most of the women's campaigning has been conducted without assistance from Lotus Place or HAN. For over 20 years, the women whose stories are featured here have been in contact with journalists, bureaucrats and politicians, seeking public recognition and financial redress. Yet, this independent action has been discounted by some members of parliament who have referred the women to Lotus Place.[76]

This pattern of referral suggests an assumption by those in power that the women *need* an institution to advocate on their behalf. Political scientist Sabine Lang notes the increasing number of not-for-profit and non-government organisations (NGOs) that have a humanitarian function or lobby for certain collective interest groups.[77] This global change is termed 'NGOization' to indicate a shift in society from a series of self-organised, broad, collective actions to a series of professionalised, managerial, marketable, 'policy-outcome-driven' services.[78] Such institutionalisation has the potential to depoliticise social change and undermine democracy. Lang's analysis illuminates the structural power dynamics that can result when advocacy becomes an industry and politicians and bureaucrats refuse to engage directly with unrepresented groups or individuals.

---

74   Lotus Place, 'Home', accessed 18 February 2020, www.lotusplace.org.au/.
75   Lotus Place, 'Historical Abuse Network', accessed 18 February 2020, www.lotusplace.org.au/getting-involved/historical-abuse-network.
76   Wendy Emond MP, letter to 'Erin', 18 December 2002; M. Weaver (Director, Executive Correspondence, Office of the Premier), letter to 'Erin', 29 November 2011; Tracy Davis MP, letter to 'Erin', 23 November 2012; Claudia Whitton (Principal Advisor, Minister for Community Services and Housing and Minister for Women), letter to 'Margaret' (Rose's sister), 12 August 2011; Tracy Davis MP, letter to 'Margaret', 10 December 2012.
77   Lang, *NGOs*, 1.
78   Ungsuchaval, 'NGOization', 2.

The experiences recounted here highlight the need for independent research on how the needs of survivors of institutionalised child abuse throughout Australia are being organised, funded and heard.

Federal Responses

In addition to state-based inquiries into out-of-home 'care', the Australian Government initiated a number of investigations, resulting in three crucial reports: *Bringing Them Home: Report of the National Inquiry into the Separation of Aboriginal and Torres Strait Islander Children from Their Families* (1997),[79] *Lost Innocents: Righting the Record—Report on Child Migration* (2001),[80] and *Forgotten Australians: A Report on Australians Who Experienced Institutional or Out-of-Home Care as Children* (2004). The last drew attention to the plight of non-Indigenous Australian children. These inquiries were preceded by decades of survivor-led struggle and advocacy.[81]

It is estimated that over 500,000 children experienced life in out-of-home 'care' in the twentieth century in Australia.[82] The *Bringing Them Home* report noted that, 'nationally we can conclude with confidence that between one in three and one in ten Indigenous children were forcibly removed from their families and communities in the period from approximately 1910 until 1970'.[83] Most historians agree that at least 50,000 Aboriginal children were stolen from their families during this time.[84] The estimate on Child Migrants from Britain or Malta is 7,000.[85] The remaining 440,000+ children were non-Indigenous Australians.

---

79 Human Rights and Equal Opportunity Commission, *Bringing Them Home*.
80 Senate Community Affairs References Committee, *Lost Innocents*.
81 The International Association of Former Child Migrants and their Families was established in 1997 and serves as an advocacy and campaigning organisation. See IAFCM&F, 'Child Migrants Trust', accessed 25 March 2020, www.childmigrantstrust.com/iafcmf. In 2001, Dr Wayne Chamley, from the Broken Rites (Australia) Collective, spoke at the Child Migration Senate Committee hearing about the need for a third report into abuse of children in institutional settings. See Senate Community Affairs References Committee, *Official Committee Hansard*, 248. The Care Leavers of Australasia Network also campaigned for a third inquiry into institutional 'care'. See CLAN, 'Past Inquiries, Senate Inquiry', accessed 22 September 2019, www.clan.org.au/past-inquiries/ (site discontinued).
82 Senate Community Affairs References Committee, *Forgotten Australians*, 29.
83 Human Rights and Equal Opportunity Commission, *Bringing Them Home*, 30.
84 For example, John Pilger, 'Another Stolen Generation: How Australia Still Wrecks Aboriginal Families', *The Guardian*, Saturday 22 March 2014, viewed 18 August 2019, www.theguardian.com/commentisfree/2014/mar/21/john-pilger-indigenous-australian-families; Lindy Kerin, 'Long Journey to National Apology', *ABC Radio*, 13 February 2008, accessed 25 August 2019, www.abc.net.au/worldtoday/content/2008/s2161585.htm.
85 Senate Community Affairs References Committee, *Lost Innocents*, 62.

A Royal Commission

In November 2012 Prime Minister Julia Gillard recommended that a royal commission be appointed to inquire into institutional responses to child sexual abuse. Out of 57 case studies considered by the Royal Commission into Institutional Responses to Child Sexual Abuse, 13 were concerned with organisations, individuals, dioceses or official processes within the Catholic Church.[86] In his narrative, the priest recounts his disappointment at the lack of subsequent and necessary organisational change within the Catholic Church, despite the recommendations of the Royal Commission. He notes that the living history of former child inmates at Wolston Park Hospital requires greater understanding of the systemic abuse perpetuated not only by churches but also by state-run organisations.

Some of the women survivors, as well as the nurse, discuss in these pages their frustration at the lack of public recognition flowing from the Royal Commission, because their testimonies were confined to private hearings. The *Royal Commissions Act 1902* was amended to enable private hearings as part of the Royal Commission into Institutional Responses to Child Sexual Abuse. Public testimonies were confined to a series of selected case studies. The women survivors featured in this book lobbied for a dedicated case study for Wolston Park Hospital as a means of gaining public recognition of their plight and their bid for financial redress. They knew that, as royal commissions in Australia have coercive power to summon witnesses, source documents and authorise search warrants,[87] a public case study had the potential to fulfil a wider investigation. However, this was not granted.

---

86   Royal Commission into Institutional Responses to Child Sexual Abuse, 'Case Studies', no date, accessed 29 September 2019, www.childabuseroyalcommission.gov.au/case-studies.
87   Commonwealth of Australia, *Royal Commission Act 1902*, s 2.

Towards a Public History

Some of the submissions to the 2003 Senate Inquiry into Children in Institutional Care, which preceded the *Forgotten Australians* report, spoke of the need for public acknowledgement of the history of childhood institutionalisation.[88] This led to Recommendation 35 of the 2004 Senate Report:

> That the National Museum of Australia be urged to consider establishing an exhibition, preferably permanent, related to the history and experiences of children in institutional care, and that such an exhibition have the capacity to tour as a travelling exhibition.[89]

The result was the National Museum of Australia's temporary touring exhibition 'Inside: Life in Children's Homes and Institutions', which opened in Canberra on 16 November 2009, the second anniversary of the National Apology to the Forgotten Australians and Former Child Migrants.[90]

Through a range of media, including objects, *Inside* represented the experiences of the Stolen Generations, Former Child Migrants and the Forgotten Australians. Preparation for the exhibition coincided with the implementation of the Queensland redress scheme. Former child survivors of Wolston Park Hospital contacted the curatorial team as part of their push for recognition and redress. The exhibition included a module that represented their narratives and also published their stories online.[91] This was not the first time that narratives of former patients at Wolston Park Hospital were featured in a museum. 'Remembering Goodna: Stories from a Queensland Mental Hospital' was displayed at the Museum of Brisbane from November 2007 to March 2008, and included stories from those who lived and worked there, including former

---

88 Senate Community Affairs References Committee, *Forgotten Australians*, 326.
89 Senate Community Affairs References Committee, *Forgotten Australians*, xxvii.
90 Australian Government, Department of Social Services, 'Apology to the Forgotten Australians and Former Child Migrants' Families and Children', accessed 19 February 2020, www.dss.gov.au/our-responsibilities/families-and-children/programs-services/apology-to-the-forgotten-australians-and-former-child-migrants.
91 National Museum of Australia, 'Inside: Life in Children's Homes and Institutions', accessed 19 February 2020, insideblog.nma.gov.au/.

patients.[92] In 2010, the Queensland Government apologised to former children under state care who were placed in adult mental health facilities, but it did not commence reconciliation talks until 2017.[93]

Goodna Girls provides spoken evidence of systematised prejudice throughout the health, education, legal and social services sectors within Australia—a bureaucratised injustice affecting those who endure poverty and hardship. The legacy of systemic abuse is written on the bodies of survivors. Some 'Goodna Girls' bear scars on their arms from self-harm during their teenage years or from cigarette burns inflicted by staff at Wolston Park Hospital when they were too sedated to fight back. Facial lines have been formed in brows that furrowed at each act of betrayal, and deepened by dehydration from physical neglect in childhood, spent tears, rough sleeping as adults and attempted relief through substance abuse. These corporeal markers are underlined by sceptical temperaments that are often slow to exhibit warmth to those in authority. These women's lack of trust of those in power is demonstrated in their refusal of superficial politeness and may, at times, be punctuated by anger. Limited formal education, unemployment, poverty and a lack of social capital are reflected in the conversational style of some of the women—speech that rarely resembles that of the middle class. One could choose to understand these signs as a means of forming a necessary armour. Instead, these physical and behavioural signs are often (mis)used to assess levels of social and economic worth, credibility, intelligence, sanity and virtue. There needs to be greater understanding of the reality that, for adult survivors of institutional child abuse, the level of distress displayed in the presence of professionals who work within the justice or health sectors is not symptomatic of criminal intent or mental illness, but is a normal reaction to the fear of further confinement.

Following on from the recommendations of various inquiries into institutional child abuse, centres have been established throughout Australia to provide services to survivors. But there is another imperative: a public history that acknowledges the breadth and depth of policies that enabled the confinement of children in the first place. A fear of social contamination and a preoccupation with mental hygiene paved the way for the incarceration of teenage girls in an adult psychiatric facility. But there is another form of cleanliness that may emerge from non-interventionist

---

92 Besley and Finnane, 'Remembering Goodna', 116.
93 Queensland Government, *Reconciliation Plan*, 3.

and open dialogue. Cultural scholars Jane Goodall and Christopher Lee advocate for greater understanding of 'the impact of traumatic memory … beyond the frame of personalised treatment'.[94] Public access to the narratives of the 'Goodna Girls' provides a means to challenge the power structures that supported this brutal history. The alternative, silencing their stories, can be likened to a form of privatisation: 'The privatisation of the public sphere like the privatisation of trauma itself threatens to constrain a liberal exchange amongst the people, which is itself understood as an imperative of personal, social, civic and political hygiene.'[95]

It has taken courage for the women in this book to disclose their personal narratives, because, too often, the disclosure of their childhood experiences has been used against them. *Goodna Girls* is thus an entreaty for a meaningful public history as part of a nation's response to the care of children—a history that should be multifarious, far-reaching, led by social justice and scaffolded by further research. In the meantime, the following pages comprise my attempt to extend the narratives that were encountered in two exhibitions (at the Museum of Brisbane and the National Museum of Australia) to inform a just resolution to a living history that, for too long, had been cast behind closed doors.

---

94 Goodall and Lee, 'Introduction', 4.
95 Goodall and Lee, 'Introduction', 5.

PART 2: THE SURVIVORS

2
The Panther: Jean/Erin

The word I use to describe my childhood is 'violent'. I was born in 1952 in Sydney, the youngest of eight children and named 'Jean' after one of my aunties. My mother handed me to my sister and said, 'Take care of this.'

Children's Homes

She disappeared but my dad was there; he died when I was two. Then I was put in Waitara in Sydney. My father was one of eight children and so was my mother. None of those aunties and uncles ever took any of us kids when we were young. They let us all go to children's Homes.

I lived at Waitara until I was three. That was when my sister Shirley got married and got me out of the orphanage. Her husband was in the army and they had permission to bring me to Queensland. Shirley had a baby, Lisa. I was three and I slept in the same room with her. Lisa died when she was a few months old. She choked in her sleep.

I used to think Shirley was my mother. I remember when I was eight, Shirley's mother-in-law said to me, 'When are you going to stop calling that bitch your mother? She's your sister.' She was a gossip and caused so much trouble. I asked Shirley why she didn't tell me the truth. She told me that she was waiting until I got older and she was going to explain to me what happened. I asked, 'Well, where's my mother?' She said, 'She's dead.' I found out that she had lied when I came home one day and she was crying. She said, 'Our mother died today.' I was shocked. 'You took away my only chance to see my mother', I told her. That was the end of my relationship with Shirley. I never saw my mother. There's not even any pictures of her because my eldest brother Frank got rid of all the photos.

I loved Richard's (my sister's husband's) father. 'Grandad', I used to call him. He was a truck driver and he used to babysit me. We used to go fishing together. He took his dog and I'd take my dog, Sparky. He was a wonderful man. He said to me after he had his stroke, 'You were a bonza kid Jean.' I think those words kept me alive.

I know that my sister Shirley was living in pain because she had lost a baby and her husband's family didn't accept her. Shirley and Richard ended up having five kids and there was no help. It was really hard. Everything they got was from junk and op shops. She'd sometimes strip me to check that I wasn't stealing, not that I ever stole anything. She took it all out on me and said that our mother left because she didn't want me. I wasn't even allowed to have friends over. She was crazy and vicious. We lived in the bush and there was no electricity. Shirley used to hit me around the head with the pieces of wood that she had for the stove. I used to have welts all over me from the ironing cord. She sometimes threw rocks at me.

She'd say, 'Get out of my sight and go to school.' I couldn't even go to the bathroom to wash the blood off me. She beat me so badly that when I went to school the teachers used to take me to the hospital. But the teachers never asked about it because back then it was different. People never interfered with other people's families. That's when I started running away. I hit her back once. I must have been about 10 and I took off. I run like hell. The police from Southport station were always looking for me. I used to go to school with the sergeant's daughter. I can always remember his name. I kept running away. He always used to take me home.

Then the government got involved and they fostered me out to a family. That lasted all of about two weeks. I didn't fit in. The mother was a good cook. She used to cook for the Queen when she came out here but she wasn't a nice person. I hit their daughter because she was telling everyone at school about my personal business. So they took me to the police station and I was taken to Tufnell Home.

Tufnell was very strict. Me and two girls went out one night. I thought it was OK to go out and we came back to the Home in the morning. My brother Robert who lived in Parkes had made arrangements with the Children's Department to take me out for the day. He drove all the way up here and he was going to buy me something and just have fun with me. But they wouldn't let me go because I'd gone out of the Home the night before. I was sitting there crying because they wouldn't let me go out with my brother. I begged him not to leave me.

My brother argued with the nuns, 'I've got permission! I've got the letter from the Queensland Children's Department!' But they wouldn't let me go. They said, 'If you take her off the premises, we'll call the police.' He got in the car and his wife—she is still alive and she is a lovely woman—said, 'I can't do this anymore.' It was heartbreaking for all of us.

When I went back inside, the head nun told me that I wasn't wanted and she hoed into me with a cane, saying, 'Stop crying. Nobody loves you. Nobody wants you.' I kept looking at the door and I'm wishing for my brother, 'Come back. Come back.' I knew that if he'd seen he wouldn't leave me there. But he never came back. I will remember that 'til the day I die. It broke my heart.

Once when I ran away, when I was 11, I met a widgie named Pat aged 15. She used to tease her hair. She went to Sydney to meet someone and I went with her. When we got to Sydney and the people she wanted to see, I didn't like them. I didn't feel safe and so I left and went up to Kings Cross. She came and met me three weeks later and we went back to Queensland but in the meantime, I met Tom. He was nine. He had run away because he used to get badly beaten by his father. He was sitting by the El Alamein fountain and we started talking. He asked me if I wanted to go to 'his place'. He slept under a church. I think the priest knew he was there because he used to leave food. We used to hang out at the Cross and sleep under the church at night. After that, Tom was on the fringes of my life forever because he was a brother to me.

Mitchelton

They sent me off to Mitchelton— a laundry run by the Good Shepherd Sisters. Some of the nuns were OK but there was no schooling for me. Wherever they put me, I caused trouble. They put me in the ironing room. I lasted a few days there and I threw the iron in the pool because only the private kids could use the pool. I wasn't allowed because I was a ward of the state. So they put me in the mangle room, which was pretty hot.

I said, 'I'm not doing that!' So they put me in the washing room. Well I wasn't doing that. So they said, 'Well, you have to go in here.' It was the packing room and I was fine in there! I worked with Sister Ignatius. I used to have to count everything that come in—see that the blue tag was for the linen from the hotel on the Gold Coast. When they went back, everything had to match that order. If it said '80 sheets', there had to be 80 sheets. I was good at that because I was using my brain. I was happy there. I found my little niche and actually didn't throw a tantrum.

Sister Ignatius taught me to type and another nun took me out to a local high school to do a typing exam. I was 13. When I come back and we were having our meal a few weeks later, a nun on one of the mics that they used to talk on said, 'Jean! Stand up.' I thought, 'Oh frick, what shit am I in for now?' She said, 'You got the highest marks in Queensland.' I got 99.9 per cent. You see, they could tell that I was a brainy bitch and they should have fully educated me but they didn't. All I wanted to do was go to school even though when I was there I was in so much trouble for hanging out the window and talking to people. But when we had the exams, I was always top of the class and the teachers would shake their head at me because I acted like I was never listening. It was too easy. Once I knew something, I knew it.

My other sister Valerie had been fostered out and that family was very, very good to her. She stayed there until she was married. One time a year, in the school holidays, her foster father would pay for me to come down on the bus from Queensland and he would let me stay at their house in Sydney so I could be with my sister. She got a job on a switchboard when they had the wire things that went in and I can remember going to work with her. On my birthday she bought me a marcasite ring and necklace but Shirley made me take them to Mitchelton so they got pinched.

I had enough of Mitchelton and so I escaped from there. What also triggered my rebellion was Valerie's wedding. My brother travelled from Parkes and picked me up to go to the wedding in Sydney. Robert's wife Liz was a beautician in a chemist and she did my hair up and my make-up. She made me really happy. I loved her. She was so kind to me. I've got a picture on my wall of that day. I was with my brothers and sisters and I didn't see them for years at a time. The next day she left on a ship for Scotland. She'd married a Scotsman. Robert drove me back to Mitchelton. I missed my sister so bad. That's when all the trouble started. I couldn't handle the pain and no one seemed to care.

I was the first to escape from Mitchelton. No one had escaped because it had rolled barbed wire at the top of the fences. I hid in one of the saints. Those statues were hollow. I shimmied up against the wall and snuck in the back of it. All hell broke loose because I was missing. They were looking everywhere. I was thinking, 'Please don't find me. Please don't find me.' After they all went to bed, I crept out. I jimmied the lock because it was old. I was outside the laundry and got over the fence, in the corner where the barbed wire overlapped. I'd already worked it out. I cut my legs to pieces but I got down on the other side.

I hitchhiked to the Gold Coast and stayed with different friends. A week later the police caught me and took me back. I had to tell the nuns how I escaped. They made me promise not to tell anyone else. I was back in the packing room for two years. If you didn't behave yourself, you couldn't go home.

I thought, 'I don't care. I've got no home to go to.' I saw one nun, Sister Maria, hitting one girl and pulling her hair. I walked over and said to her, 'Stop doing that!' She turned around and started pulling my hair. Big mistake. I wasn't going to let her attack me. I pushed Sister Maria in the pool. Everybody ran. They had the police come and take me off to Karrala.

Karrala House

I saw the fence with the barbed wire and behind it was a building in a U shape. On the right side were all the solitary cells. At the bottom were the doctor's room, the sewing room and an office where the nurses sat behind unbreakable glass. On the left-hand side are the rooms where you slept at night and you were allowed out of that room during the day. There were nine rooms on each side.

When you arrived everybody got put into solitary first because you were punished for whatever you did before you were sent to Karrala. There was no conversation about how I felt. No one spoke to me as a human being. You were just a thing. They already knew everything about me and just told me what to do. They showered me from head to toe, looked me over everywhere and made me put on striped pyjamas and then stuck me in a dark room for 19 days. The bed was a slab attached to the wall with a hessian bag on it. No pillow. There was a black potty. Nothing else. I was 14. I thought, 'What the hell is this place?'

They let me out in the morning to have a shower and empty my potty. I cried for days after they cut my hair. All the light switches were outside and so I was in the dark, unless I had a nurse who felt sorry for you who would turn your light on for a little while. Occasionally you would get a good one like that but you got no sunshine. There was no tap in the room for water. Some were mean and they wouldn't feed me—instead of getting three meals a day, you might get one. I never ate the cereal for breakfast because it had crawly things in it. There was no radio, no noise and I didn't know what day of the week or what time it was.

I remember this huge spider in the room. It was dark but I seen it when the light was on and I must have screamed for about three hours, 'Nurse! Nurse! Nurse!' No one came.

After 19 days I went to the other side—the 'good side'—of Karrala House. I actually had a bed there but we didn't have sheets. There was a stripy mattress, a pillow and blankets. On the 'good side' they let you out of your room during the day but you still weren't allowed to speak to anyone. Girls were aged between 13 and 15. You spent all day in the sewing room and it's where you had your lunch. Everything was done in silence. It drove you crazy! Karrala was in the middle of a mental hospital. No other patients were near us but we did the sewing—making pyjamas for the other patients. We worked on the sewing machines all day. Now I hate sewing. I start shaking if I have to sew and when I sew a button I make sure that it will never fall off. If it's got two holes, there's a big bulge in the middle where I've gone back and forth with the thread because I don't want to do it again.

Karrala was tough. It was like back to nature—survival of the fittest. A lot of people thought we were in Karrala because we were bad. No we weren't. Most of us had absconded from Homes. We weren't bad but they made us hate. They always used to give us milk and cake for supper. One night they gave us burnt cake. I have never seen such black cake in my life. It was like black shoe polish. I wouldn't eat it. I put my hand up. It was my turn to speak up. We got payback—punishment—from the nurses for speaking out so we took it in turns. It was my turn to complain this time. I asked, 'Can we leave the cake? It's burnt.' They said, 'No. You have to eat it.' I asked again. They still said 'no', so I picked up the plate and threw it against the wall. Then everybody did. Cake was flying all over the joint. The warders got there so fast. So it must have been a set up because warders usually had to go through two sets of gates but this time they were there in a few seconds. They grabbed me, took me to solitary, to Room 9, which had nothing in it—just a potty but no bed. Room 9 was called 'POP', meaning 'Place of Punishment'. They stripped me naked and left me there for five days. They had given me such a hiding. I'm sure they cracked my rib because I was in pain for a long time and I still have scars on my bottom lip where my teeth went through from being bashed that day. If you were in that room, you'd lie against the slits in the door so that the staff couldn't look in, switch the lights on and see you naked. All the girls used to do that in Room 9.

I would yell out to the other girls in solitary. We tried to speak to each other. Sometimes, to pass the time, we would sing the songs we had heard before we came to Karrala—'Needle in a Haystack' was one of them and every night Barb used to sing 'Paper Roses'. She had a beautiful voice, that girl.

I had medical examinations all the time but I only think I saw a real doctor once. I had to put my legs up and they did whatever. Then after that, the male warders would come and take you there and do the physical examinations. Some girls were put into solitary for refusing to have a medical examination. Everyone knew this was going on because when the men came and got us we walked past the nurses' station and so the nurses saw it.

I can't prove it but I think we were being given some kind of medication. They used to give some girls pills but they refused to take them and so there were no more. We then figured they must be feeding us drugs some other way and we guessed they were in our food. I don't remember having my periods when I was in solitary. On the 'good' side, where you were let out of your room during the day, they gave us towels to use—like white hand towels but smaller. You had to use safety pins to keep it in place. After you used it, you had to wash it in the sink in the hallway. Under the sink was a white bucket where you put your towels after you washed them. They took the bucket to the laundry. But there were no sanitary towels or laundry bucket in the hallway in solitary.

My sister Shirley visited me once but they stuck us in a room with a hole in the wall and someone sat on the other side and listened to everything that you said. One day I got up in the morning and went to go to the day room and I seen my clothes and I thought, 'Yes! I'm getting out of here!' They sent me back to Mitchelton. By this time, I hated every adult walking the earth but I didn't hate other kids. I had a foul mouth and I couldn't settle. I was sick of being locked up. I wanted to go. They said that I was disruptive. Well, I just come out of Karrala—of course I was disruptive! I got into a lot of fights. I'd lost my humanity from the cruelty and the coldness of people. You can only bash someone so many times until they turn around and start to hate. I could feel the hate in me. So they sent me back to my sister's and she went back to her old tricks—bashing me and carrying on so I ran away. The cops got me but the sergeant at Southport Police Station was so nice to me. He used to give me food.

He'd say, 'Doesn't anybody feed you, you skinny little shit?' The police would put me in the cell at the back and leave the door open. They knew me. They'd come and talk to me. There were kind people in my life. I remember them and try to hold onto that. The Southport police got the call from Brisbane saying I had to go to back to Karrala House and they'd say, 'No. We're not driving her. You come and get her. We're not taking her to that place.' They wouldn't take me to Mitchelton either. It was the Brisbane police who took me to Karrala. When I got out of the car, I knew where I was. I still remember the despair that I felt. If I could have got hold of the policeman's gun and shot myself, I would have done. I thought, 'I can't do this again.'

What did they do? 32 days in solitary. How's that? That was the punishment for running away from my sister. I used to sit in my cell and think, 'What did I do?' There was a nice nurse at Karrala who used to leave the light on for me in solitary. I asked her for a book to read. She gave me *Uncle Tom's Cabin*. When she went off shift, she'd have to come and take it off me. She'd say, 'I'll give it to you again tomorrow.' That's how I got to read all of it.

I also went to my meadow about a hundred times. It was the 'place' that I would go to while I was in solitary. There were trees and flowers in my meadow. On the edge was a waterfall. There was a little girl there. Of course I knew who that little girl was. She and I would swim. When I had to leave the meadow, I used to cry because I didn't want to leave her alone. So I created a big black panther for her. It came over the hill, down to the waterfall, sat beside her and put its head on her lap.

After 32 days they let me out. I was only out for a couple of days. Solitary was supposed to break your spirit but I came out really, really angry and so I was trouble. I wouldn't sew. I would argue and the mouth on me was like a wharfie. The thing they held over you was, 'If you don't behave yourself, you don't get to go home.' Well, I didn't have a home and so I didn't have a reason to behave. They pushed me that far that I didn't care anymore and I was put back in solitary.

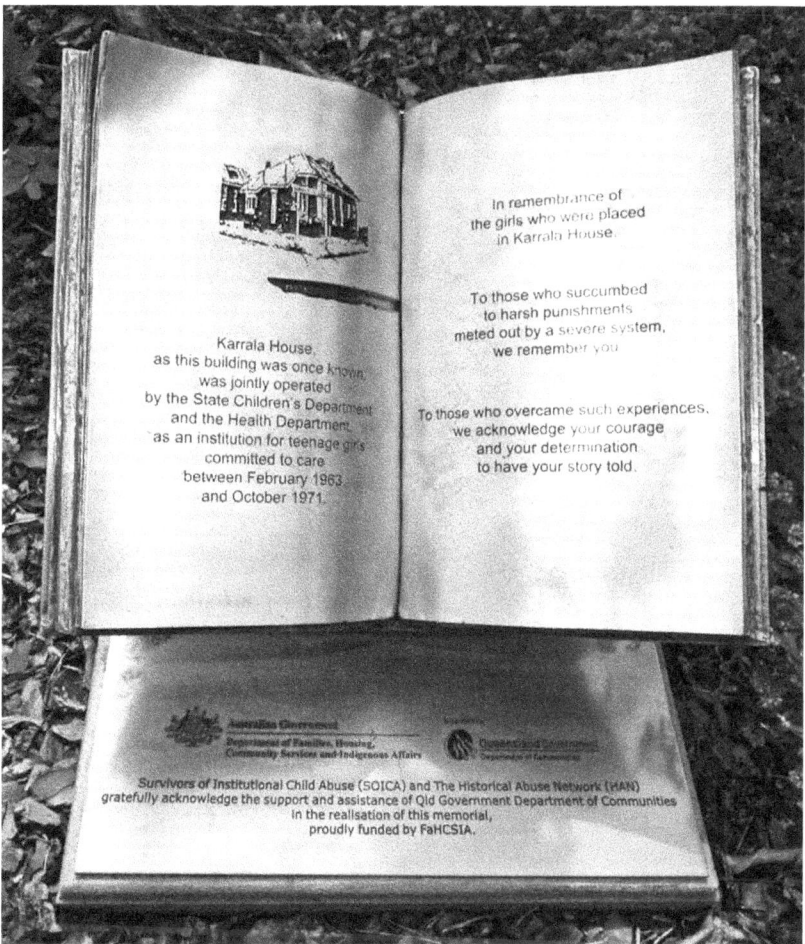

Figure 1: Plaque dedicated to former inmates of Karrala House, c. 2000.
Source: University of Queensland.

Lowson House and Wolston Park Hospital

I was then transferred to Lowson House in Brisbane Hospital because they said that I swallowed a sewing needle, but I hadn't. It wasn't true. In my files are my X-ray results, 'No foreign object found'. They lied at Karrala House. They just wanted me out because they only wanted those that they could control. Lowson House was a locked ward with about 10 beds. It was my first meeting with the crazies but they were sedated so they weren't too bad. They told me I was neurotic and they gave me pills.

I was in Lowson House for about 10 days while they were finding out about my mother. After they found out that she was dead, a social worker signed me into Wolston Park. Where did she get her medical degree? They took me there in an ambulance and I was taken to the admissions ward where there were adults in hospital gowns, doped to the eyeballs. I was locked in a cell at night and let out in the ward during the day. Everyone was docile. It was such a nothing in my life, that ward. No one tells you anything. You go and see a doctor but they've already got you on pills, so when you see a doctor, you don't know what he's talking about. There was one doctor who wrote to the Children's Department, trying to get me out. But other doctors were at me with their fingers and pressing my breasts. I don't know what that had to do with psychiatry! I was 16. I didn't know where I was.

I didn't last long there. At the back you could walk out onto the verandah and there was a lawn that went off into the bush. So muggins here takes off! But I didn't have any shoes on and there'd been a bushfire through there. Have you ever walked on spiky grass? I was running on that. Frigging hell, that hurt. I got to a road and the first car that come along was a nurse. I hadn't even left the premises. I was still in Goodna so they took me back.

That was my first go at Ward 8. I was an absconder and so they couldn't let me out for two seconds. I spent most of my time in Ward 8 for the criminally insane. You just looked at them and they were dead. They didn't have feelings for themselves or other people. There are two types of people—if you get caught by one type you can kiss your arse goodbye and if you get caught by the other lot, you can talk your way out of it. These people were like the first type. There was one other young girl in there, about my age and she was nice.

I'll never forget Ward 8. It was the worst thing ever. There was one old lady there and she used to bite and spit. At night they put her in a padded cell. They let her out during the day in a straightjacket and nothing else on, and they'd tie her to a canvas chair. That's where she'd sit all day. There were no books, no TV, no radio—nothing. Two patients tried to kill me. One had her hands around my throat and I saw the madness in her face. She was so strong that I blacked out. The nurses got her off me. After that, I sat with my back against the wall. I still do, everywhere I go.

One day I was in the bathroom and there was no nurse there. One patient grabbed me and held my head under the water in the bath. There was just one second where she loosened her grip and so I headbutted her. I had blood on my head from her teeth.

In the shower there was a cement floor and no curtains. All the patients were naked and they would touch me. And the male warders would wash me from head to toe.

I was starving and dehydrated. There were no taps in your cell. Meals were a joke. Other patients would take your food or throw up in your food. We were all given Valium at mealtimes. And there were heavier drugs. Haloperidol was to calm you down. Paraldehyde was to knock you out. Once I was given Haloperidol and then the nurses on the next shift came, a half hour later, and gave it to me again. They overdosed me. It's in my file—there's 'Haloperidol' with 'OD' and a question mark written next to it and the instruction, 'Keep walking her'. They nearly killed me.

I remember one time coming out of drugs in my cell and there was a fella on top of me. Another time I woke up with cigarette burns on me. Once, two male warders came in and after they finished with me, one turned to the other as they were leaving and said, 'We have to thank the government for sending us all these pretty young things.' An hour later somebody came in with a mop and a bucket, called me a dirty bitch and told me to clean my blood off the wall. I couldn't tell anyone. There was no-one to tell because everybody knew already what was going on. I was also threatened with, 'There are a lot of "suicides" in the Bremer River.'

My sister Shirley came to visit me there once. I got on my hands and knees and begged her to get me out. I never begged anyone for anything but I did that day. And fancy begging her for anything! She said, 'I can't. It's out of my hands.'

I was frightened of becoming like them—the other patients. One of the nursing sisters, Sister Allen, was really nice. She knew how bad it was for us young kids. She worked nights and she let me out of my cell and let me sit up with her and the nurses and we would play cards. Every night after midnight the male warders would have to go out of Ward 8 and do something else and that's when Sister Allen would say, 'Go and have your shower. They won't be going in there.' She organised it so that I had privacy. Before she left at 6 o'clock in the morning, she would lock me in my cell after giving me an injection of Paraldehyde to knock me out during that day. When she came on at night, she'd come and let me out. She could see what was happening to us young girls but she couldn't stop it, so she protected us the only way she knew how. She said to me when the male warders weren't there, 'We know you shouldn't be here.'

I was becoming a wreck. I was really skinny. I was shaking and my hair was falling out. They then sent me to the ward where they did the shock treatments. I never had it but I did see other patients have it. They'd bring patients in from other wards, tie them down to the gurneys and gave them mouth guards. Some patients after being brought in realised where they were and they would try to run. Some hid behind me and begged me to help them. I always get upset about those patients because they were so afraid and they asked me for help and I couldn't help them. The more shit I seen like that, the more I hated the world.

On the Run

I decided to leave one night because this wasn't a secure ward. Before that I had got information over time because I knew I was going to leave. I had asked the nurses—just in conversation—where I was, in what direction was the next town, where do you get the bus to work? I'd worked it all out and I escaped at night, went off into the bush but I ran into the biggest spider's web. I was covered in web from head to toe.

Then I got into town. This fella on a big Harley motorcycle pulled up and said, 'You escaped from that place. There's a cop car around the corner so you better hop on because they'll grab you dressed like that.' I took a chance and jumped on the bike. He turned out to be one of the nicest guys I ever met but you wouldn't want to see him down a dark alley. He'd scare the living shit out of you. He had a beard and tats and everything but he was such a nice man. He took me to his place and he fed me. He got takeaway food. It was nice but I was sick. That place had made me sick. I didn't realise it at first but I learned that being at Wolston Park had made me an addict from being fed drugs all the time. I was shaking and I was throwing up. He used to bring me stuff to make me feel better—some dope to smoke and stuff on bits of blotting paper to put on my tongue. I couldn't survive without it.

He said, 'I got someone I want you to meet.' He brought this girl around. It was Jan who became my best friend ever. She was a trained psychiatric nurse. She was about 20. Jan wanted to travel around Australia but she needed someone to go with her. He helped us and we got backpacks. Jan cut my hair and blonded it and changed my name to 'Erin' and the same surname as hers so that we could pass as sisters. I got a bank account in my new name. You could do that back then because you didn't need all those

IDs. My name was all over the Queensland radio because the cops were looking for me. Jan told me all about her family, her address, everything and I memorised it all.

We earned money when we needed it by going on the game—to get money to get drugs. Jan was on drugs too. When we were broke, we'd get off our faces with mixing milk and whole containers of nutmeg. Being on the game was no different than what the male warders were doing to me at Wolston Park, except on the game, the men behaved better. They were respectful. We hitchhiked.

The American sailors had come over from Vietnam. They had the good dope to smoke but they didn't have a never-ending supply. They were looking for girls. We would hook up with the sailors who had dope. Jan knew of this stuff—tobacco for asthmatics—that you could get from the chemist. We would put in a matchbox, pretend it was marijuana and sell it to sailors for ten bucks. We'd smoke their good gear first. By the time they got to smoking our stuff, who the hell cared what it was?

We hitchhiked and when we were outback, near Charleville, two guys pulled up and gave us a lift. Both their names were 'John'. We arrived at a motel and they got two rooms. They said that we had to sleep with them. We thought, 'Oh god!' They had these four pennies, which they threw to work out who was going to sleep with who. We were hoping that there were locks on the bathroom doors! They threw the pennies—Jan and I got the tails and they got the heads! We made them stick with their word, so Jan and I got a room to ourselves and they got the other room! The next day, they were travelling to do something—they were salesmen, something to do with farming stuff. They get to where they're going and we arrived at another motel. They said, 'Tonight we're not throwing pennies. It's happening tonight, right?' The car had barely pulled into the driveway and Jan and I took off. We were gone.

We got inside a slow train out west somewhere. When we got out it was dark and this copper pulled up. He was only a young fella. He told us hitchhiking was dangerous and took us home to his house and gave us tea and everything. It was nice. Nothing happened. He was nice. The next morning, he dropped us off. In another town, we got pulled up by the cops. I showed them my bank account and answered all their questions about who I was in the way that Jan taught me. They let us go and we decided to go south, to get out of Queensland because I was 'wanted'—this big, bad escapee from a mental home—good lord!

We hitchhiked to Broken Hill. We had a tent and got caught in a sandstorm. We lost everything just about, so we ended up in Melbourne. Jan got a job as a go-go dancer. I was underage and working as a waitress in the same bar. I lost my job when the fella who owned the place found out how old I was and Jan left with me. Then we both got a job working together knocking on people's doors selling orange juice, in the middle of winter. Then we got a job in a biscuit factory and we were the only two that spoke English so they wanted to make us bosses! We didn't want the job because I had itchy feet. I didn't want to stay anywhere. Plus, if you stay anywhere, you get caught. We were living in Fitzroy in this boarding house. Jan got a job around the corner in a coffee shop. I was talking to this man I met in the street. He was nice. We had coffee together. His mates seen him speaking to me. One night they came and did terrible things. These guys knocked on the door and grabbed me. I seen the guy I knew and he put his head down. I'll never forget. He put his head down.

When Jan came home and seen what had happened, because I was a bit of a mess, she said, 'We gotta get out of here.' We went to Sydney. We slept in a deserted, condemned house near the El Alamein fountain in Kings Cross. Other people lived there too. One night this man came at me with a knife. I hid in a wardrobe. Next, there were cops running around. Jan and everyone had run to the cop station. They got him. Jan said 'We're going to Queensland.' I said, 'I can't go to Queensland.' Jan said, 'I gotta get out of Sydney. Those people that are after me are still here.' Jan had been in Sydney before she met me and she was in bad trouble. It all had to do with drugs.

Back to Wolston Park

I took my chance and I got caught, didn't I? Back to frigging Wolston Park. Coppers picked me up in the street in Brisbane. I'd been away for six months. Back to Ward 8. Barb was there that time. The girl who was in Karrala with me. I loved her. We were best friends. She always laughed, no matter how bad it got. But I went back to the drugs they were giving me, men showering me, warders touching me, patients hitting me.

I got a visitor. They said it was my brother Robert. I ran out and it was this person I'd never seen before. I yelled out, 'Hi Robert!', and I'm thinking, 'Who the hell is this guy?' The guy said, 'Jan sent me to tell you that if you can get away, she's working at Gladesville Psychiatric Hospital.' I said, 'OK! Thank you!'

I was deteriorating. I was becoming an empty shell and there was so much pain. The staff were vindictive. If they did come into my cell to see if I was awake, they wouldn't shake me—they'd kick me in the head. They broke my eardrums. I was bleeding from the ears. My hair was falling out. My teeth were green. I think the staff could see how bad I was. I was a wreck.

Over the Border

They sent me back to my sister Shirley's place just for a week. I went to my sister-in-law's and asked her to give me a dress. I got on a bus and went south to New South Wales. The people who were after Jan had moved on so she was back in Sydney. I went to Gladesville and stayed in the nurses' quarters with her. One night we went to the Ball Pants coffee shop in Kings Cross where they played folk music. There was a guy behind the counter who was gorgeous. He—Bill—came and sat down and we talked. I went home to his house and I stayed there for 13 years.

One day Bill came home from work and he caught me and Jan shooting up. He threw a tantrum. He told me, 'You get off it or you get out!' I loved him that much that I went cold turkey. He had time off work and he was with me while I went through all the shit.

When our son, Will, was born he was taken from the hospital before I left and placed with another family. I was 19 and Bill and I weren't married and if you were a single mum they just took your baby off you and adopted them out.

Bill is a Maori man and when Will was born, a nurse said to me, 'I see you have been fucking black fellas!' I was so tired and upset that I didn't say anything. They put Will on the other side of the room so that I could not see him. This young nurse came in, picked him up and on her way out of the room, quickly came over and gave me a quick look. I could see she was so sad herself because of what she had to do. I did not know they were going to take him away until I had come to the hospital to have him. There was nothing I could do. I couldn't even run or tell his dad. We would have run away somewhere. I felt anguish and despair. This on top of everything I had been through at Wolston. But because Will's dad was 24, he went to a Chamber Magistrate and demanded his son back. We got him back about five days after I left the hospital.

Jan went to Perth but came back and stayed with us one night, after I had the baby. The next day she went and killed herself. She jumped off the cliff at the Gap. When she stayed over, I didn't pick up on it. The police came but I couldn't go to identify the body because I was only 20 and so Bill had to go and do it. Jan had written a letter before she died and posted it to me. It came after she died. She had tried to get help getting off drugs. She had flashbacks all the time. I'm still angry at her for doing it—my best, best friend.

Bill and I went to get married when I was 20. We went with the baby to Births, Deaths and Marriages in Sydney. I had to get permission because I was still a ward of the state until I was 21 and I was still on the run. I said to Bill about the baby, 'If they grab Will, you grab him and run. Don't ever look back to me. I'll take care of myself because if they get him, we will never see him again.'

We filled out the forms, sat there, ready. The magistrate called us in and said to me, 'You're wanted.' Mate, you never seen two people go to that door so quick. The magistrate said, 'Stop. Stop. It's OK. I read some of this stuff. I'm not going to say anything. But you're 20 years old. You'll be 21. Then go and get married.' He let us go. We went home, packed up and moved.

I was naive. Bill got a DUI fine in Bondi—$400. Every week he would give me the money. I'd go up to the post office and get a money order 'til it added up to $400. A month later, the police knocked on the door and wanted to arrest him for not paying the fine. He looked at me, 'What were you doing with that money I was giving you?' I said, 'I paid it. I got the money order. Look, I've got the receipts.' I showed them the money orders but I hadn't sent them anywhere. The police laughed at me, took the money orders and left. This is what the government did—they didn't teach me how to live!

After 13 years, Bill got too big for his britches. He started playing up with women and gambling. He just went nuts. There was Will to think of. I got a place and I gave Will what I never had. He played sport and his friends came round to our house. And my friend Tom, who I met in Kings Cross, when I was 11, he was like a brother to me and 'Uncle Tommy' to Will—he would help. A friend got me a job at Sydney Uni, clearing tables at the cafeteria. It was only three days a week and four hours a day to start with. I had to walk to and from work because I had no money for the bus. When the girls found out, they were putting food in my locker for me to take home to feed me and Will. Another lady there used to give me clothes when her son grew out of them. Then, I worked my way up, running the food outlets at the Bosch, where all the medical students go. I was there eight years but it was term-only employment.

When I was working at Sydney Uni, I was working under an assumed name so it wouldn't affect my pension. I don't know why the government is so stupid—you go to social security for a review—back then, the single mother's pension was $300 a fortnight. My rent was $290! Nobody ever woke up and said, 'What are you living on?' So when I got a part-time job at Sydney Uni, I wasn't out buying blocks of units or cars—I was living on it.

When Will was 14, there were a lot of bad things going on in Sydney. His mates were getting into trouble. I was on my own. I felt out of my depth and so I come home. Bill, my ex, had found this stupid girlfriend and one night when him and her were drinking, he told her all my business. She went to social security and dobbed me in—said I was working on the pension but my friend's sister worked there and would throw the report in the bin. She knew I had no money but the girlfriend went into the office and told someone else. I had moved up to Queensland by then but they got me up here. Will was 17. The day I went to court I had a job at the Gold Coast City Council, to start on that day but they gave me eight months' jail. The judge asked the prosecutor, 'Has she got a criminal record?' 'Yes. She does, as a teenager.' I'm thinking, 'No. I haven't.'

Boggo Road Gaol

I was sent to Boggo Road Gaol for stupid social security fraud. Everyone who goes there goes to maximum first. I was there for a while. I sat on Table 8 with a woman who'd killed a child. A screw said, 'You're working in the kitchen.' The screw was happy that she had someone in there for non-violent crimes that she could put in the kitchen. I said, 'Well, I'm glad someone's happy!'

It was still OK because I wanted something to do. The other girls said that if I wanna live, I was never allowed to speak to the child killer. They did all sorts of terrible things to her meal. I said, 'I'm not going to do that. That's not who I am but I will never say a word about it.'

The prison dentist took out all my rotten teeth—oh, the stench from my gums—stitched me up and gave me false teeth. When I got out of max I had to organise the deliveries of food and bread and make sure that they went to the right sections. Every time you go through a gate, they search you, almost to stripping.

So one day I went down there without any under clothes on and I'd just lifted up my dress. And they'd say, 'Jean! Jean! Put your clothes on!' I said, 'Why? You just want me to take them off all day!!' And you're forever carrying messages for people. I had a slit in my shoe where I'd put notes.

There was this girl who decided she liked me and all the time she was putting her hands on me. One day, she caught me with the big trolley choc-a-bloc full of milk going down to the max gate. She was going off at me and I could see her fist. I knew by the look on her face that she was going to belt the living shit out of me so I hit her first because I knew damned well it was the only punch I was going to get. She broke my nose. Milk went everywhere. Screws came running out, 'What happened here?! What happened here?!' She's looking at me and I'm looking at her because I could have got her put away. I said, 'I fell over.' She left me alone after that.

There was another woman, Kay, in there for computer crimes. She shouldn't have been in max. She was out of her depth. At least I'd been through Karrala and Wolston. She was a young, nice girl. She used to hang with me all the time. There was this other huge girl in there. When she was in solitary, she'd put big huge dents in the steel door. One day Kay came running into the kitchen and hid behind me. Then in came the big girl. I thought, 'Oh my god!' I'd been through this before in Wolston Park. I know when someone wants to kill me. I looked at the pot of boiling water for the potatoes and I said, 'If you touch me or her, I'm going to throw this all over you.'

She left because I stood up to her and the day I was released she called out, 'Erin!', and gave me the thumbs up.

As I was leaving this horrible nurse said to me, 'You'll be back! You'll be back!' The screw who was standing next to me answered for me, 'This one? No she won't.' I make a good impression everywhere I go!

Bearing the Cost

I had got out after four months, on parole. When I got out of jail, I found out through freedom of information what my juvenile record was because I knew I didn't do anything wrong. My juvenile record was 'charged with being neglected' but the prosecutor hadn't told the judge that and so he thought that I was a bad person. The prosecutor lied. People don't tell the truth and they don't understand about Forgotten Australians.

I was working in a fish shop and the government was ringing me saying I had to pay the pension money back. They told my boss that they were going to take my wages. I objected. I got the court records and found where the judge had written, 'No restitution.' I said to them, 'You can't have the money and the body.' They've changed the law now. If you go to jail now, you still have to pay the money back but this was in 1988.

I'm an insomniac. I won't take sleeping tablets. I sleep with the lights on. I don't like darkness. I can't stand any doors in my house being closed. The memories they left in our heads; we should never have them. After my son was born, when it got to September, every year, near my birthday, I became petrified. I was fearful for my son because I had this feeling that I was going to die and he would be put in Homes. When I got the records, I found that the 32 days that I was in solitary at Karrala started on 1 September until 2 October—two days before my birthday. I still get anxious in September but I'm not fanatic about it, now that I know why.

I was talking to my local doctor at the time—she was in her 80s. I found out that she used to work at Lowson House. I said, 'Oh really? They had me in there when I was a child.' She asked, 'When?' I said, 'In the '60s.' She was there then, I'm pretty sure of it. You should have seen her face. She never took me as a patient again. She backed right off. She never had me back.

It's hard to get a decent doctor. When you explain what's wrong with you and they ask why, they don't believe me when I tell them. A doctor told me once to get out of his office and stop lying. About 10 years ago I found a good doctor—an ears, nose and throat fella—because I had an ear infection.

He looked into my ears and said, 'What the hell happened to you? No one looked after you when you were a kid. Do you know how much scarring you've got in these ears? You must find it hard to hear.' He was so nice to me. He said, 'If I can fix that, I will and I'll do it for free.' He was upset. He sent me for so many tests and I never paid for any of it. When I went back, about a month later, he sat there and he had tears, 'I can't help you. It's so bad. You'll end up deaf. There's so much damage. It's unbelievable what they did to you.' I've learned sign language.

Tom, who I met in Kings Cross when I was 11, had rheumatic fever when he was about 12 and was left with a hole in his heart. They said to him that he would never live 'til he was 21. I don't know what the hell for they're telling people this. He walked away from the girl Christine who he loved because he thought he was going to die. And he lived until he was 58. He never married. Anyway, he led a wild life. He never broke the law but he was a wild boy. He was a forklift driver and moved up to Queensland in 1986. He was family. I taught him how to read and write. He was a smart fella. He just hadn't gone to school. He loved my son and his children and he was part of our family. We loved him. Him and my family all call me 'Morning' or 'Morn' for short, because that's how I would greet everyone each day. He was 'Uncle Tommy'. I sat with him in the hospital while he died. The last word he said was 'Morn'. I've got his ashes. I had to move heaven and earth to get them. The state was just going to give him a pauper's burial.

I have a funny relationship with food. I was hungry for years at Karrala House and Wolston Park. There'd be arguments over food because everybody was hungry. I was talking to a doctor about it once and he said that there's an old saying, 'If you've ever really been hungry, then you're never full again.' That describes my life. I have to eat everything on the plate. I can't waste food. I can't throw food out. Even if I'm full, I have to eat it. I don't enjoy eating and I very rarely eat in public. I don't do it anymore—Tom got me out of the habit—but I used to hide food in the house. I used to overfeed my son. I had to stop that.

I found out the other reason why they took me away from my sister. It wasn't only because I was running away. Two years before she died she said to me, 'I owe you an apology. I accused you of stealing. I found out later that you didn't do it.' I said, 'Let me guess how you knew. Whoever was doing the stealing was still doing it even when I wasn't there!'

I later read a letter in my files, which she had written to the government asking them to take me away because I was stealing. Nobody asked me. I went through all those years and all that suffering and I didn't do it. I got punished for something that I didn't do. Shirley found out later who really was doing the stealing—taking money out of her purse. It took me years to understand Shirley's life. Before she died, we were mending fences but we just didn't have enough time. She was also molested, by an uncle. The week before she died I asked why she always hated me. She said, 'Because when Lisa choked, you should have woken up!'

Ken Blanch, a journalist from the *Courier Mail* did an investigation into Karrala House in 1967 but he didn't know about Wolston Park. He said no one ever told him. No one at Wolston Park had the guts to tell him what they were doing to us kids. They could have tipped him off anonymously. The story could have come out in 1967. Instead, it wasn't until 1996 that it all came out in the newspaper. After Ken Blanch wrote the story in the weekend paper about children having been locked up in mental institutions, a survivor asked him to publish her post office box details so that other survivors could contact her if they wanted. Ken printed the address in the next week's paper. Some of us sent letters to it. From that, eight of us got together. Only three of us from that group are left. The rest have since died. We've been fighting for 20 years. We're dying off. No one cares—hey!

We would meet in West End, in Brisbane. Some of us were members of SOICA—Survivors of Institutional Child Abuse. Then came the Forde Inquiry in 1998 and I spoke to the inquiry about being in Tufnell and Mitchelton. I was allowed to speak about Karrala, but only very, very lightly. When I talked about Wolston Park, they turned the recording off because it wasn't in the terms of reference. In 1999, after the Forde Inquiry, we kept in touch. The best counsellors for us are each other because only another person who was there knows. I know other counsellors try but it's platitudes they say at you. It's what they've learned out of a book. I think, 'You have no idea what I'm saying to you. I'm trying to tell you something.'

Some of us were visiting each other and we were going to different lawyers. This was all new and I think most didn't believe us. I rang an advocacy group and all of us had a meeting with them. They found lawyers for us who did 'no-win, no-fee' but it was early days. Everyone was naive. They also found us a private detective who did background work for us and didn't charge anything. A law lecturer from a university also came on board. So they started a class action against the Queensland Government for the eight of us Wolston Park survivors. There were more survivors that we met later but at this stage it was just us. Our lawyers had to try a single test case to see if it would get past the time limit on how long you could bring something to trial after the event had happened—it's the statute of limitations. If the lawyers could get one test case through, then they'd go to court for the other women. The test case was me. I didn't want it to be me. I don't know why it was me. The only reason I can think why was because I lived in the street next over to the lawyers' office! Why didn't they use someone who was in Wolston Park more recently?

It took so long to get to court. We went to Brisbane. The lawyers presented my evidence—my personal records of my time in Goodna. The rest of us sat against the back wall. The judge turned the case down because of the statute of limitations. He said that the opposition—the Queensland Government—couldn't defend itself because it happened too long ago. But he said that our lawyers could argue in terms of fiduciary duty—the government's duty of care. It would mean another hearing. I was really upset afterwards. I felt that I had let everybody down.

One of the government lawyers who was defending the State of Queensland saw that I was shaken up and came up to me and said, 'If there was ever a case that I wanted to lose, it was this one. But you were never going to win. That judge is a good friend of the premier of Queensland.' We didn't get a decent hearing. That was bullshit!

The government lawyer gave me his card. Later I rang him to get a transcript of my test case because I didn't have the money to pay for it through the normal channels. He was really nice to me. I've met a lot of nice people. A couple of days later, the court transcript arrived in the post.

Then nothing happened. That law lecturer was supposed to present papers to the court so that we could leave our case for the issue of fiduciary duty and he never did it! So I can never get my case heard again unless we get permission from the court. That lecturer buggered things up for us. We would need to get a lawyer to go back to court and argue that it wasn't our fault that the case wasn't left open and to argue for another chance. We were very naive back then. I'm mad at the legal system. It's only for the rich. It's not set up for poor people who usually have crimes committed against them so it makes you a victim—a victim of the legal system. It's expensive to get all you need to go to court. We each had to pay for a psych report as evidence of how Wolston Park affected us.

However, later, a similar case did get through the courts—for a woman who had been in Karrala House. Because she had the old punishment book from Karrala as evidence, the judge let the case go through without worrying about the statute of limitations because the time limit is discretionary. It's not a law. That woman got a payout. It was a different judge than ours.

I don't trust the legal system and I don't like the way we've been treated in all the inquiries. I also rang the nuns of the Good Shepherd, asking them for my pay for working two years in the laundry and they said I was doing 'work experience'! Don't you love that?!

My son Will had a partner but she took a hike when he got sick. At 22 his brain tumour came. When he has blood tests, you see on the paperwork, 'Reasons for tumour – Haloperidol'. That's one of the drugs I was on at Wolston Park. He'll never get better. They won't operate. He's 44 now and no doctor will give him clearance to work. His two sons, aged 18 and 22, are very close to their dad.

What they did to us back then was so cruel. What sort of people were they trying to make? I want what they took away. I would have owned my own home. I would have been able to visit my sister in Scotland. I want a home for Will because he's sick. He can't work. I don't want him worrying about rent.

What they're doing to us now is so cruel. We've been fighting this for 20 years, trying to tell people what they did. We're still fighting. Nobody listens. They don't have any idea. They just push us aside like we're nothing. It's like we're an annoyance. I write a letter to a politician. I take a day or two. They send me back these form letters as if I'm nothing. They don't answer the letter I wrote. It's like I'm not important. It's the same feeling as being in Wolston Park. No acknowledgement. Why do my fellow Australians hate me? I've had a wasted life. I could have done so much. It was all taken off me. I give them the credit of having brains by taking the time to write a letter.

I've always felt intellectually alone because my life has never been what I could have done. I used to be able answer all the questions from those quiz shows on TV when I was 16. I like Greek mythology. I read everything—about five books a week. I like the author Sven Hassel—all about the Second World War. I'm an online gamer. I'm number 26 in the world. My friend in Romania with a major in economics, she's number 27.

I said once, 'My way of looking at this earth is that the strong have to help the weak, to make their lives better. Whether you're a boss or a parent, you have to pull people up.' The looks I used to get from people, so sly and horrible, so you pretend you're stupid, then, 'When did you get so smart?' I'm starving for intelligent conversations.

In the mid-1980s, I went through the phone book to find my relatives. I rang them and I found a cousin, Jan, and I met her mum, my aunty who I was named after. Jan said that they couldn't take me and my brothers and sisters because there were eight of us. I said that there were only four of us that went to Homes because the rest were grown up. I got a call from a cousin who remembered me as a kid. He said, 'Do you know that your mother's Aboriginal?' The first I heard about it. In 2015, one of the staff from Lotus Place looked up the records and confirmed that it was true. She was a Wiradjuri woman from New South Wales. I reckon that's why all the photos went missing. I reckon my eldest brother got rid of them because back then it was bad to be Aboriginal.

My brother Robert and sisters were here many years later and we were talking and I said, 'You know how the youngest in the family is supposed to be the spoiled little bitch and gets everything she wants? Well, when does it start?' My brother looked at me and gave me a big hug.

We need the government to admit that back then, what they did back then, was a big, big mistake and to ask, 'What can we do to fix a little bit of it?' I look in the mirror sometimes and I can see that girl from Wolston Park. I can see her green teeth and balding hair. I see her looking back at me.

I love panthers. I've got pictures of them on my wall. I've got a soft toy panther on my bed. They're so strong, independent, solitary, solid. A couple of years ago, I heard about a litter of cats on the way to the pound and of course I had to look, didn't I? I chose a black one—my very smart mate.

3

One of the Most Persistent Bitches: Judy

I was about one and a half when, in 1946, I was put in the Queen Alexandra Home and my sister Gloria must have been about seven and my other sister Beverly was nearly four. My brother was born just after that. I was the first one put in the institution. I lived there until I was 12 years old. My mum had walked out on us—her four children—and dad served in Japan during the war. He sent money to the Home, about 14 shillings a week, for the whole family.

Queen Alexandra Home

My first memory—me sitting in a cot with my foot all bandaged up because I had stepped on a nail. I remember it being so funny, me throwing my food at other girls. There was a Mr and Mrs R. there. They wanted to adopt me and my dad wouldn't sign the paperwork. I can remember my sister Beverly and there were people we used to call 'Matron' and 'Sir'. My brother was never put in there. He was adopted out to other people.

Queen Alexandra Home was a huge building full of tiny children. There were private wards and state ward children. Still to this day I can remember the front entrance and the black and white tiles. I can't walk into a house that's got black and white tiles. I have to get out of it. There must have been 100 children in there. Sir and Matron were pretty brutal to us. There was a bottom dormitory and there was a dormitory upstairs when the girls got a bit older and there was a small boys' dormitory at the top of the stairs next to the Matron's and Sir's quarters. When they reached a certain age, they were sent out of the Home and put into another institution. One of our aunties worked there. There was probably about seven or eight staff altogether, including a cook, a gardener and the guy that chopped the wood up for the big wooden stoves in the kitchen. My father wasn't allowed to visit me at the Home.

There was just no compassion shown to us. The beatings we got were absolutely shocking. They had this thin piece of bamboo and they used to take your pants down and whack you with that or there was the strap that they used to sharpen the razor and they'd belt you with that. I was only little and they'd belt you with these sort of things. It affected me because they would—and I think that this is psychological cruelty—make us line up and we used to stand for sometimes two hours, waiting to be belted.

Can you imagine what that does to a child, the waiting and the thinking, 'How bad is it going to be this time? How many belts am I going to get?' And for absolutely nothing. Just nothing. They were so sadistic, these people. They seemed to get their jollies by being cruel to children.

A 'Mr Q.' came there and he was a dirty old bird. They had baths up on the big old concrete blocks and we used to climb up on the concrete blocks and had to put our little legs up over to get into the bath and the gardener used to stand at the louvres and look through the windows and Mr Q. used to come in to bath us and he made a point of watching us between the legs and we'd have to get out and he used to stand there and watch us. I reckon he was just a dirty old bird. They were very cruel in there. They were very cruel.

On the street, there used to be a stand where you'd buy newspapers. We used to up-end it and take the money out so that we could buy lollies. We'd have to go to church every Sunday morning in Coorparoo and we'd walk past this beautiful big mulberry tree and, of course, mulberries—we never got fruit or anything like that and the owners of the tree would give us a punnet of mulberries and say, 'Here's a shilling, go get some ice cream.' And of course we'd go Home and they'd say, 'Have you been eating mulberries?' And we'd say, 'No.' But our mouths were purple and so we got the shit belted out of us. For what? And it was the constant hunger. The porridge in the morning would be full of weevils. I am lactose intolerant and they would make me drink milk. I couldn't stomach it and they would make me vomit it up into the glass and re-drink it every time I vomited it up. And to this day I can't touch anything with milk—custard, anything.

Figure 2: Queen Alexandra Home, Old Cleveland Road, Coorparoo, Brisbane, c. 1950.
Source: State Library of Queensland.

We were always so hungry. In the morning before school we used to go into the cake shop and they knew we were Home kids and they'd give us the old cakes because they knew were we hungry. We'd bring them back and we'd hide them underneath bushes and we'd tell the tiny, little kids where to go and get the cakes.

The Coorparoo State School was right next door to us. We were always called the 'Homies' and that has stuck with me all my life. We were always differentiated. We were below everybody else and the teachers never bothered try to explain something if you didn't know it. No one cared. You either knew it or not. We virtually never got an education. When my sisters reached a certain age, they were taken out of the Home and put in Wooloowin and were told that because Beverly and I played up that Gloria was going to be put in a lion's den. Now you don't go and tell that to two little children. That's just horrific and I never saw my brother.

Foster 'Care'

We were going to Mrs S.'s every weekend. She lived at Yeronga and was a committee member of the Methodist Church. In the end she asked if she could foster both Beverly and I. Beverly never liked her because she was so cruel and Beverly was terrified of storms. She would make Beverly stand outside in that storm and Beverly just up and ran away. So I was there on my own.

Mrs S. was a religious freak. That's why I'm not religious. I don't think that we were any more than slaves for her to do the work that she couldn't be bothered doing. When I was 12 I was handed a push mower, mowing this huge property that she lived on. In those days, they only had boilers with big wooden pegs. I was a little girl and I used to have to lift that stuff out of that boiler and put it into cold water. Then I would have to put it through a hand wringer that I could hardly move and then put it out on a line and they had big wooden sticks to lift it up. I would then have to bring that in and do all the washing up. I had to do the work around the house. That's all we were—slaves. If I did something wrong, I would be locked in that bedroom. I wouldn't get a skerrick of food. I would have to walk to school—no lunch, nothing—and then walk home from school of an afternoon and I'd be locked in that bedroom without any food or anything. That woman used to thrash the living lights out of me. Mrs S. was a brutal woman. I don't know why they had to be so brutal. She used to get absolute pleasure by belting me. She'd make a cake and it would go mouldy and she'd cut the mildew off the cake and I would have to eat that. I can remember so bloody much. None of these people from the institutions realise that we have got such bloody good memories—'never forget'.

She had a boyfriend and I would come home and I would find them behind the door, fooling around with each other and I just used to get the shock of my life because I'd never seen anything like that in my life. I was a very naive little girl.

My dad would come to Mrs S.'s and he was so drunk that she just told him to get out of the house and then he came to the school one time. They rang the police and took him away. I had constantly been told that my dad was a dirty old man and that he didn't really want us. They made me terrified of him.

While I was at Mrs S.'s she went down to St Mary's in Sydney for a holiday with her boyfriend and left me with the bloke over the road, Mr L., who molested me every opportunity he got. She must have known what he was doing. At that age, all I knew was the institution. It was something that you never said anything about in those days. If you told anybody that someone was molesting you, they'd beat the living shit out of you. You just didn't talk about things like that. On a Tuesday night we used to go to the movies and Mrs L. used to put bright red lipstick on me and rouge on my cheeks and she used to put little heels on me. It was as though she was grooming me for him. I went to the police station at Inala a year ago and told the policewoman about the sexual abuse and they investigated it. They found out his name but he died when he was 91 years of age and so there is nothing that can be done.

I ran away from Mrs S.'s in the dress I was in. No shoes. Nothing. At the time I was working. They got me a job in a book depository. Now I never had an education. Why give me a job in a book depository where I had to deal with paperwork and that sort of thing? I had no education.

All the time they'd threaten, 'If you lose your job, lose your job, lose your job, we're going to put you in another institution.' I was terrified of going to another institution. I was also a nurse's aide at an old people's hospital. I used to really enjoy it. In my files it says that I was asked to leave because I became 'too rambunctious'. That's an out-and-out lie. I left the hospital because I got a job at another hospital. I wasn't over the top. I was a shy little girl. Mind you, I'm bloody well not shy now! But my hospital work stopped when I ran away from Mrs S.

Absconding

I got on a bus and I ran away to my friend Helen's. She went to the same school as me. I went to her house and stayed there for about three nights. Her dad said, 'She can't stop here any longer.' So Helen said, 'Look, I'm going to have to take you to Stones Corner. You should be all right there. You'll meet somebody there who'll help you. You'll be all right.' Stones Corner was a suburb where the bodgies and widgies used to hang around. Helen was a bit of a widgie and her brother was a bodgie. He had a motorbike.

But I'd lived a sheltered life. I didn't know what to do. I was hanging around Stones Corner and I sat at a bus stop and it was right near a car yard and I tried the car doors and got into one of the cars and slept in the back of that, that night in the car. The next morning—I was used to getting up and washing my face and that sort of thing—I went down to a toilet and this bloke was standing there and he said, 'What are you doing?' I said, 'I'm going to wash my face'. He said, 'Well come into the men's toilet and if you need some money, I'll give you some.' And me being so naive went in there! Some people had seen it happen and rang the police. The police come and said, 'What are you doing here?' I said, 'He told me he was going to give me some money.' They said, 'We think you better come with us.' They told me they were going to take me back to Mrs S. I said, 'No! I don't want to go there!'

Kalimna

I thought my sister was at the Salvation Army and so I said to the police, 'Will you take me to the Salvation Army please?' So they took me to the Salvation Army to Kalimna at Toowong. In my paperwork it says while I was at Stones Corner that I was promiscuous. I didn't even know what the word 'promiscuous' meant. They took me in, early in the morning, and I was put in a cage. They let you out to go to the toilet. There was a Matron. there who was also the local member in government. Dr C. was the doctor who came in. When you were taken to Kalimna, you were physically examined. They didn't tell you what they were going to do. He put your legs up and he put one of those things inside. I'd never had anything like that done to me in life, apart from that bloody bastard who lived opposite Mrs S. Dr C. was just so brutal. It was as though they did everything in their power to hurt us young girls. No need for it. Afterwards, I bled for 10 days solid. What right did they have to do that to a young girl?

Matron wrote in my records that I ran around the dormitory at night and kept the girls awake. I was never admitted to the dormitory! I can't believe these Christian people could tell so many blatant lies! I was let out of that room twice. Once I went in to have breakfast and I can even remember where I sat. There was tables and chairs all around the room. There was a stage and I sat at the end at the left, and then another time I was taken down to the rec room where the girls used to sit and I was down there for half an hour and they put me straight back into the room. In my files it says that I was talking in a smiling way about committing suicide. I would never commit suicide!

I was locked up all the time. I was 15. After the cage they put me downstairs. If you were 'uncontrollable', they put you down in the isolation ward where there were six cells. They were all staggered so that we couldn't see or talk to each other and it was called 'POP' (place of punishment). There was a mattress on the floor and we had no toilet. They would take us for a shower in the morning, breakfast in the room, if you could call it breakfast. We'd be let out to go to the toilet three times a day and when the sun went down we had no lights in the room and that's where I stayed the whole time. I just lay on the mattress. Do you know how agonising that is to the soul of a child? It's just cruelty, out-and-out cruelty to children who had done nothing wrong, absconded from something they didn't like. I'd been sexually abused by the neighbour of the foster woman and I was angry about that. They said I was running around dormitories at night. I never went near them! There were also girls who were up in dormitories. I got out twice—once to have breakfast one morning in the red room. It was a long table and the girls sat on forms at the table.

You could yell out to each other but they'd tell you to 'shut up' or give you more drugs to shut you up. It was just hopeless. You were drugged up the whole time. These people were supposed to be religious. Matron was a liar. I can't stand liars. I think this is why I'm so outspoken because I don't believe in lying. Whatever I say is the goddam truth all the way through and I do not suffer idiots. I don't care. I've got to the stage of not worrying what people think.

Salvation Army promotional brochure *Kalimna: Lovely Home* (1963)

3. ONE OF THE MOST PERSISTENT BITCHES

KALIMNA—

A TEXAN was once endeavouring to impress a Queenslander with the size of his State. ' We have trains ', said he, ' in which you can travel all day and all night and still be in Texas.'

' I understand, ' said the Queenslander sadly. ' We have trains like that as well.'

Leaving aside considerations of public transport, the fact is that if you double the size of Texas and then add New Mexico or Montana for good measure, Queensland will still be larger.

Or if transatlantic measurements leave any old-world reader cold, then add Western Germany to France, to Italy, to Spain and to Portugal, and the resultant area reaching from Hamburg to Cadiz and from Bayonne to Brindisi will still be slightly less than Queensland.

Now place a pin point in the south-eastern corner of this immense area. Let this represent the one and only Protestant home for delinquent girls in the whole of the State, and some small idea will be gained of the sphere of operations of ' Kalimna '—an aboriginal name which means ' lovely home '.

The work of The Salvation Army for girls in Queensland, and particularly in the state capital of Brisbane, goes back to 1886. A domestic house in the inner district of Paddington was the scene of modest beginnings, and a year later the work was transferred to larger premises in the nearby suburb of Milton.

GOVERNMENT GENEROSITY

In 1896 a more commodious dwelling was secured on the outskirts of the city at Taringa, but early in 1914 this was burned down. Then followed the purchase of a timber house at Toowong, and this old building—adapted and altered and readapted and realtered—served the purposes of this redemptive work until last year when ' Kalimna ' was built at a cost of £140,000, the State government generously meeting 75 per cent of the capital cost.

As the pictures will show, nothing lies like an institution could be conceived. A broad stairway from a quiet street leads up to an inviting doorway at which the Matron, Major Jean Geddes, awaits any interested visitors who may call. The flow began even before the Home was officially opened—students taking a social service course at the university, the Mother Provincial from Melbourne, welfare workers from the United States, officials from other State children's departments, government representatives from Colombo specializing in work with sub-normal children in Ceylon. And well they might come, for General Kitching observed on his own visit this year that he had seen only one other building of its kind in the whole world to approach it.

But behind the pastel shades and delicately tinted drapes there is a passion to redeem the girls who are in residence, all of whom are between fourteen and eighteen years of age and have been committed to the Army's care by the children's courts. All have been, or were, in danger of being involved morally. The means for their cure is expressed in the lay-out of the building itself, as will be seen as the Matron takes visitors around.

LOOKS BELIE

By the way, let no one suppose that the Matron's lack of inches indicates any lack of capacity to deal with any emergency which may arise. Said one distinguished visitor at the opening of the Home in November last: ' I expected to see a tall commanding lady.' What counts in Matron Geddes is measured from the shoulders upward. Twenty-five years of experience with human nature lie behind those friendly eyes—as more than one turbulent girl has discovered on arriving at the intake suite which lies to one side of a pleasant and roomy grassed courtyard.

CHALK PROVIDED

' Suite ' is perhaps the only word which adequately describes this self-contained unit with all modern conveniences which can house five girls. Fastened to each bedroom wall is a small blackboard. Chalk is provided below. The temptation to inscribe *graffiti* on the walls magically vanishes when the means to write on an appropriate part of the wall is provided. Morning light has been known to reveal a list of boys' names chalked on the blackboard, or at other times a prayer: ' O God, let me go home on Friday.' But the desire to go home diminishes as the new girl realizes the delights of her present home.

Along the courtyard from the intake suite lie the craft rooms—the sewing-room, the commercial room, the beautician's room. Under expert tuition the girls learn to make their own dresses. To be taught typewriting without expense is a chance which does not come every teenager's way. And, as every girl wants to look her best, the visiting beautician teaches deportment and dress sense.

GOODNA GIRLS

At right angles to the craft rooms and flanking the far side of the courtyard is the gymnasium. Showers are conveniently adjacent, and again both body and mind benefit from skilled training. Full marks should be given to the voluntary experts who freely visit the Home in their spare time.

PRIDE IN SURROUNDINGS

The middle section of the Home takes twenty-four girls, and it is to this series of three-bedded rooms that the newcomer is transferred in due course. Each girl has her own built-in wardrobe and set of drawers. Each bed has its own bed lamp, and the delight and comfort of these rooms are such that a girl begins to take pride and pleasure in her new surroundings. This is reflected in the care which she bestows upon her room and its contents, for each girl knows that misconduct could mean relegation to the intake section once more.

The final stage is when a girl is promoted to one of the twelve single rooms in the hostel section. From here, if necessary, she can go out to work during the day and in the evening return—not to her old neighbourhood where the odds were weighted against her, but to the unforced, unsanctimonious care of the officers who have shown her such affection and for whom she has conceived a genuine affection in response. For many of these girls this place stands for their first experience of being loved for their own sake and of being able to return that love without fear of the consequences.

Of course, behind the seemingly effortless running of this attractive Home for sixty-three girls lies an immense amount of work. The Matron can be called upon by the State children's department, by the police, by distraught parents—and by the girls themselves at any moment of the day. The resident officers live not for themselves but for these delinquent teenagers. They both share and supervise in the laundry where the girls work in order to help to meet the bread and butter expenses of the Home.

'Kalimna' could not live up to the meaning of its name without the Christian faith—accepted not as an arid dogma but as the presence of a living Lord.

Sunday mornings see the girls sharing in the holiness meeting at the nearby Toowong corps. Family prayers are held each day in a pleasant meeting hall whose glassed wall overlooks the entrance steps. Here stands the Army flag—the only visible religious symbol—with its significant colours.

The assembly hall also provides a meeting place for an evening's entertainment. At the movement of a shutter a cunningly concealed canteen opens its inviting counter. Here tea can be served and here also can be purchased the knick-knackery dear to a girl's heart, for each has a credit standing to her name through marks gained for good conduct and good work.

But the severest discipline of all is for a girl to be forbidden the swimming-pool. In a city where the average annual temperature—that is, taking winter as well as summer—is 60 degrees and the average maximum is 78 degrees, a swimming-pool is as much a necessity as a luxury. Tantrums rapidly abate when the penalty is known to be—no swimming.

FRANK QUESTIONS

It might be said that this short description gives too rosy a picture of life at 'Kalimna'. Each girl has her individual problem and most often she is her own biggest problem. With these girls their stay in the Home often constitutes their first contact with folk possessing a genuine personal Christian experience. Much of their past life has wrongly taught them to be wary of religion. Do-gooders are regarded cagily. But before long they realize that the richness and variety of life which they have been seeking at such dubious sources and in such questionable ways is spontaneously present in the lives of the young women officers who live with them from dawn to dusk. Frank questions are asked and frank replies are given. A dawning appreciation of the Christian faith is awakened in the hearts of these young girls through the blessed infection of the lives of those who themselves radiate the beauty of Jesus.

About this service three things may be said. It is unspectacular and, by its very nature, cannot be publicized in detail. It is—in the phrase of von Hügel—costing. But its effects are lasting. Here is fruit that abides.

A SALVATION ARMY SOCIAL SERVICE
(Reprinted from "ALL THE WORLD," July-Sept., 1963)

3. ONE OF THE MOST PERSISTENT BITCHES

Left: The Governor of Queensland, Sir Henry Able Smith, who opened the home, unveils the commemorative plaque at the entrance of "Kalimna."

This beautiful property in Queensland provides the new environment for the Army's work for delinquent girls, which is described overleaf by General Frederick Coutts and which began as long ago as 1886.

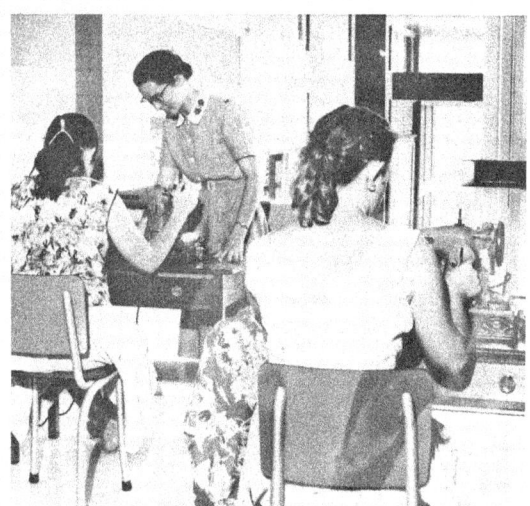

Above: A sewing lesson under expert tuition.

Left: The swimming pool in the grounds.

Issued by the Public Relations Department, T.H.Q., Sydney

Lowson House

Then all of a sudden, they just came down and got me and they put me into Lowson House in the Brisbane Hospital and I stayed there for 10 days and then they put me into this big cage—Ward 16—which was full of people that were really mentally deranged. I can remember sitting in a corner on my own. They never told you a thing. No explanation. Not a thing. There were about 20 patients in there and mattresses. I can remember sitting in a corner on the floor for hours on end being terrified out of my life because these people were severely mentally impaired. I was absolutely terrified. They were mental. They were screaming and yelling. They were being violent towards each other. I'd never seen anything like that. The way these people carried on. Now I look back on it, they were more to be pitied.

Nobody came near us. I think I saw my caseworker, Miss S., once. She came and saw me once. It was very flippant. She'd say, 'Are you coping?' There was no inquiry into what was going on.

Goodna

I was in Ward 16 at Lowson House for about three days and then they just took me. They came and got me and I didn't know where we were going. I had no idea. They took me out to Wolston Park. They called it 'Goodna' then—Goodna mental hospital. They took me into the Barrett Centre. Dr Barrett was in charge. Everyone knew what Goodna was. At school we'd talk about it. All the nutters lived out there but I never thought I was going to go up there.

I was first taken into the admission ward. Now for some strange reason they kept me in the admission ward for six months because I think they realised that I wasn't mental. There was absolutely nothing wrong with me. I retaliated at being constantly institutionalised. That's all that ever happened to me. I was placed in institutions. I was nothing. I was a little girl. I hadn't done anything wrong. I hadn't committed any criminal acts. I wouldn't put up with crap. I think that I've always been like that but not so much as I am now.

I'd see them hurting patients and I would say, 'Why are you doing that?' In the middle of winter, I saw them put old women in icy cold baths and they had these big wooden boards over the top and locked down on the baths and all they'd have was their heads sticking out and these old people would cry, 'Please help me. Please help me.' We couldn't help them. What could we do?

There was one elderly woman. I thought she was old. I don't know how old she was and they picked her up by the hair and her hair came out. And there was blood running all down her face and they were kicking her and punching her. And I actually broke down. I can always remember that. And they put me in isolation because I got upset at what they were doing to this elderly woman. She'd done nothing.

I think that we—for all our abuse—were compassionate towards other children and other people who were abused. We spoke up for them—us girls who were out at Wolston Park. We tended to stick up for people who we thought were being mistreated. At Queen Alexandra Home, as we got older, we used to defend the little ones. We'd take them under our wings. Even aged 10. I used to think I was a big girl at 10 but I was still only a child myself, but we would try and protect the little ones. If we used to see someone picking on the little ones. My sister used to do that for me.

I think I was put in Goodna because I wouldn't conform to what they wanted me to be. I think I've always been a very determined person. I don't like unfairness to people. I can't stand people being unfair. If I see somebody picking on somebody, I have a go at them. I say, 'Do you enjoy what you're doing?' I've got to the stage where I don't care anymore if people think I'm not a nice person. I've been told, 'Someone's going to hit you in the gob one day.' And I say, 'Yeah, but they'll leave that person alone, won't they?' I've become like this.

I wasn't badly treated when I was in admissions at Goodna. We just used to sit out on the front verandah and you could see cars and people walking along the road. There were still big wire fences around admissions. I couldn't come and go as I liked but I thought, 'Oh this is good. At least I'm not locked up in a bloody room all day and fed drugs.' I could walk out to the front and sit out there and watch the cars go past.

Then, out of the blue, they took me through this gate and they had these big keys and they unlocked the door and they put me in this end ward. I didn't have as much freedom. I'd say there were six or seven young girls in there at the time aged between 11 and 15 and we could sit and talk. We'd say, 'What Homes have you been in? How come you're in here?' Most of the girls had absconded from Homes. The only place I absconded from was Mrs S.'s. I was in that ward for about 18 months. I was 16.

I had told one of the nurses, 'I'm thinking of running away.' She had said to me, 'If you ever get out of here, come and visit me. I'll look after you and cover for you.' She gave me her address and told me to keep it hidden.

Then some tradesmen came in and left tools behind and so I took a screwdriver and I undid the screws on the wire on the windows and another girl and I escaped. When I ran away, I got out to Ipswich Road, hitched a ride and went to the nurse's place. She got me a live-in job with these two women who used to go out each night working. I used to clean their house and look after their kids. I found out later that they were prostitutes. There was this bloke who would come and visit the house. The nurse introduced me to him. He was about 18. He paid me attention. Anyone who paid me attention seemed nice to me because I wasn't used to anyone caring or taking notice of me. I just soaked it up. I started going with him. I also got in contact again with my friend Helen. This bloke I was with had a motorbike and he took me over to her place. Her brother had a motorbike too. I'd never been on a motorbike in my bloody life. So we all ended up going for a ride. We went down this street at night. The blokes didn't realise it was one-way and they hit the end all of a sudden. The bike fell over and landed on my leg. I got up and couldn't walk. They took me to the Brisbane Hospital but they didn't do anything—just gave me a pair of crutches. The bloke I was with took me back to his place and I was in so much agony. I went back to the hospital the next day and this time they put plaster on my leg. That bloke had been going out with one of the women in the house but he left her to go with me. She was jealous so she dobbed me into the police for breaking out of Goodna. So the police come and got me. I had been out of Goodna for a couple of months.

This time they sent me to Ward 8 with the criminally insane. There were mostly adults in there. They were poor buggers but it was also called 'J. D. Ward'—juvenile delinquent ward. There were only about four or five of us girls in there. There was a big garden out the front where you'd have your visitors, if you ever did have a visitor. At the back there was a big caged-in area with chairs that they would tie us to. And there was a part up the end where they would put the really severely mental patients where they were tied down to the chairs and they would piss and they would crap just where they sat. On your left there was a dispensary and then there was the big dining room and there were very narrow windows that you could see out the front. Right to the back of the dining area there was the kitchen. There were about five girls' rooms and there was a dormitory opposite the single rooms and up the end was the bathroom. At the end where I slept, you could see out onto the verandah and they would come and bolt the shutters up every night and lock you in the room and you were in the pitch black. I can always remember a young girl named Andrea and another called Carolyn.

In Ward 8, I told the nurses that I was very itchy and having discharge. They put me up into the hospital part. That bloke had given me venereal disease. I didn't know anything about it until then but there I was in hospital with gonorrhoea and my leg in plaster. I can remember them sticking needles into me and taking me backwards and forwards to the general hospital. I was ostracised because I had venereal disease. I haven't had it since, but in those days, if you had it, you were a dirty, dirty person. It was there that I reckon that they gave me shock treatment because I know all about it. How do I know all about shock treatment? How do I know the room where they did it? It was in a red building across from Ward 8. I knew how they strapped you down and tied your legs up with leather straps, how they put things in your bloody mouth and held you down. How did I know all that? I don't remember them doing it but when I was let out I tried to put it all behind me, but when they brought it all out in the Forde Inquiry all these things came back to me. For the inquiry we had to write over and over and over and over again about what had happened to us. I don't think that was fair. I think we should just have been able to say to somebody once what happened. We just had to tell it over and over again. I got on with my life and tried to put all of this behind me but they brought it up in 1998. Brought the whole lot up again. Brought the most horrible pain back. I had got on with my life. I travelled. I nursed. I went to New Zealand. I lived in England. And then I came back here and I had my son and I got on with my life. We women from Goodna find it very hard to show love to people, to our own children.

At Goodna, we got given drugs every morning, every noon and every night. They'd give you Largactil and on a regular basis you'd get Melleril. You look up the side effects. It was like Valium to keep you quiet. When we were given Paraldehyde, they would strip us naked and put a straightjacket on us and we would have our head pulled back and they'd stick the needle into the muscle of your leg and they were supposed to put it in very, very slowly but they just used to push it in our legs and you can still feel the pain of it. Once I say 'Paraldehyde', I can taste it in my mouth still. It would come out your body the next day. You'd constantly have the smell of Paraldehyde. It was white, thick stuff and absolutely agonising.

And my god—the abuse, the abuse! These dirty old bastards. These bloody men. They would call the male warders over to hold us girls down while they injected drugs into us. I'm sure these people went home to their family at night to their wives and children and I'm sure they went to church on Sunday morning and were told what good people they were, but in the meantime, they were molesting these little girls, raping little girls. They just did what they liked to us. I was under the age of consent. They had no right to touch me—filthy bastards. The trouble was, we were in such a zombie state from all the drugs, we couldn't remember who these people were.

And then you'd have the showers that had no doors on them, and the toilets had no doors on them and they would stand there and at that age you are so embarrassed. You are just starting to mature. You don't need dirty old bastards like that talking about you. The male warders would say, 'Look at your little titties. Look at your little pussy.' It was so embarrassing. You didn't only have to contend with them but also with the patients. I can picture that bloody woman at this table. There were four chairs. I sat on one chair and there was somebody on my right, somebody opposite and the chair on the left was vacant. Well, she would stand up on the chair and would jump across that table and batter the living shit out of me and they wouldn't move me. I said, 'Will you please move me?' They thought it was funny.

They said I would put on an act because I couldn't get a light for a cigarette. I never smoked! And where was I going to buy cigarettes? The nurses locked us in single rooms at night to protect us from the mental patients. Someone told me there was a woman in there who had slashed her children to death with a machete. Why would you put a child in with people like that?

The nurses would stir the patients up to bash us up. If you wanted to go to the toilet you'd just wee in the corner. And straightjackets? I think I lived in a straightjacket. And when they put the straightjacket on you, they would tie you down to these big canvas chairs and if you wanted to go to the toilet, you just wee'd there, and some staff would stir the patients up to bash into us. The so-called nurses, doing their training, weren't nurses' bum holes. I don't think one of them had a day's nursing experience in their bloody life. They were only young girls that would come in and apply for jobs at the hospital. They'd have a sister in charge but mostly only very young girls.

I miscarried twice in my twenties. The doctor asked if I had tried to have an abortion because the baby that I lost, when I was six months pregnant, was so badly mangled up. I put that down to the drugs that were injected into me when I was younger—Largactil, Melleril, Paraldehyde.

I was in Ward 8 until I was 18. Altogether I was in Wolston Park for three years. When I turned 18, my dad knew that I was no longer legally under state care. My dad found out where I was and sent my two sisters to come and get me. We sat out in the garden and they said that they didn't know I was in here. Dad wasn't allowed in Queensland because he owed money for us being in institutions. The State Children's Department wouldn't let him come near me.

My sister gave me a gold crucifix on a gold chain when they had come up to see me. The nurses ripped the cross and chain off me—just ripped it into bloody pieces. They stirred up a young girl to come and bash me. That was precious. I never had anything nice in my life. And to get that chain from my sister was absolutely precious because it was mine! And they made a point of ripping this chain and crucifix off my neck and bash me up because I was leaving and they said, 'Oh she's going out next week.' The trouble is the girls had been told that they would never get out of there alive. I believe Carolyn is still in there. When my sisters visited me again, they asked me where my crucifix was and I told them what happened to me. I got out of Wolston Park two weeks after them coming up to visit.

Sydney

The woman from the Children's Department came and got me out of Wolston Park, took me into shops in the city, bought me some clothes because I had nothing. I had no shoes—nothing. I virtually walked out of Wolston Park with absolutely nothing. You never owned anything.

I'd never had a normal bra because the woman I was boarded with, Mrs S., used to make me wear flat things and little shoes and socks like a little child. She wouldn't let me grow up. But Miss S. bought me little training bras and a pair of brown desert boots and a blue dress.

Miss S. took me to the airport and I had to walk upstairs to get to the plane to Sydney. My two sisters picked me up from the airport down in Sydney. My sister Beverly had been in a Salvation Army Home in Queensland after leaving Queen Alexandra and she escaped and hitchhiked to Sydney to be with our other sister Gloria. But when Beverly got there, the police picked her up and put her in Parramatta Girls Home. I know she was sexually abused in there. The trouble was, they were now 'working girls'.

My father had brought my brother down to Sydney and they put us in a flat at McMahon's Point. I got a job at Randwick Private Hospital as a nurse's aide and I got sick to death of that, paying the fares from North Sydney over to Randwick every day. In the end my sisters told me not to bother doing it, that they'd support me and my brother. We used to go down to Luna Park every night and dance to the jukebox. My brother then disappeared off the scene.

My sister moved to Bondi and I moved with her and she got me doing the same as her in the end. We used to stand on the one corner at Kings Cross down William Street. We all had rooms to go to in Surry Hills where we worked from. We rented them from elderly women and that's how they got extra money. I never liked it. I had an aversion to people touching me. I did it for a few years until I fell pregnant with my son through what I did for a living.

My son's going through a really bad time at the moment and a friend asked me, 'Do you think it's come through your childhood?' And it made me start thinking. He's incapable of showing feelings to anybody the same as I was.

With my first pregnancy, I didn't even know that I was pregnant. I hadn't been out of Wolston Park long. I was living at Bondi and I wasn't working at the time. I was in a relationship with my eldest sister's boyfriend. I must have been 18. She found out. We've never really been close since. He paid attention to me and I never had that before. I fell pregnant to him but miscarried. I was lying on a bed and my water broke and I didn't know what was going on. I'd never been told anything. I went to the toilet and I flushed it down and I didn't realise.

Later these four blokes found out, through Beverly, about me being with my sister's boyfriend. She hung around with a lot of bad people. She's never had the smarts. These four blokes came to the house and one of them left because he knew what was going to happen. These were bad, bad criminals. They grabbed hold of me, pointed scissors at me and raped me. They hung me, naked, out of the window. The flat was on the tenth floor. The next morning Gloria took me to the police. They examined me and everything. I had to go to court over one of them. His solicitor brought up in court all about me being in Goodna. He came down hard on me. They even asked Dr B. from Goodna to go down to Sydney to give evidence against me. Before the hearing they had sent me to another psychiatrist because I'd been to Goodna. The psychiatrist said in his report that for all of what I was, I was a real prude and that I was only on the game as a means to an end, to be able to live. It was all in the paper about me being a prostitute. It was an embarrassing time for me.

But I had one of the jurors come up to me and shake my hand and say to me, 'You're a really strong girl, aren't you? You wouldn't take any rubbish off that solicitor!' That rapist got 15 years. The case against the other two came up later when I was in England so I couldn't testify against them.

Travelling

I ended back with my sister's boyfriend. We went to England together. I was 26. When we were living in Middlesex, I applied for a job as a nurse's aide but I wanted to do my training so I applied and went into preliminary training school two or three times a week but I was only on the wards. I did three months' geriatric, three months' paediatric, three months' surgical, three months' emergency. I became a registered nurse and worked at the hospital for four years but then I separated from the man I was with. I was pretty distraught and so my dad paid for me to come back from England. The man I was with was playing up on me when I was on night duty and got a very young girl pregnant and ended up marrying her. I didn't want to do the nursing anymore because I was just so traumatised by what that bloke had done to me. I wanted to leave England because I had nobody there for me anymore. I came back from England and I was staying with my sister Beverly at Maroubra in Sydney and I got a job in a factory making toothbrushes. There were a lot of Pommies working there and I just came back from England and I wanted to mix in more with English people but I was only being paid a pittance and I thought about going over to Western Australia. I went over to Hay Street in Sydney to a brothel and my sister Beverley said that she'd like to go to Western Australia with me. Well I couldn't say no to her and so she came with me. But I knew there'd be trouble. Beverley's always been trouble. Well it ended up to be true. She caught a disease and they threw her out of the brothel over there.

I bought a car over there so we drove back to Sydney. I had to pay all our way back to Sydney and she ended up with nothing. I'm known as a tight-arse and I'm quite happy about that. We drove back together and I got stuck on Parramatta Road. I was so angry because I'd never driven in traffic and Parramatta Road! My god! It was just unbelievable. Someone stopped to help me and saw that I had Western Australian number plates. They asked, 'Where did you come from?' I said, 'Out of my mother's cunt!' They helped me start the car and we drove back out to Maroubra.

Back in Sydney

I chose to move out and I heard about a unit through a friend of mine. I rented that and a girl named Gloria moved in with me. I got into a brothel at Kings Cross. There were too many wild parties in the flat where Gloria and I lived and the neighbours complained and so a heap of us went and lived in a big house in Neutral Bay. We all put in for the rent. That was a very exclusive suburb. I don't know how we got that house!

Then I went back to work because I needed the money and I fell pregnant through that. Nobody told me anything. Nobody told me about periods. Another bloke, who I was with, gave me money: 'Go and have an abortion.' I took the money and went out and bought baby clothes. I wanted a child. I wanted something that was mine. My dad was around at the time and he asked if I was going to adopt the baby. I said, 'No! I'm keeping the baby!' And my dad got the shits, y'know. It was my baby! I wasn't going to give it away. I had it done to me. I wasn't going to do it to a child of mine!

I was back on the game in Sydney even when I was pregnant. I know I shouldn't have done it but I did. I told the bloke I was with that he was the father, but he wasn't. I know that sounds terrible. Anyway, he kept me. He paid my rent and my food. I met him through being on the game. He always used to take me back to his place and he said that he'd prefer me not to work. He wanted me to just be for him exclusively and so I did it. It was worth it for me. He was a very wealthy businessman. I moved into a house in Bondi Road and Beverly moved in with her two kids and brought all her junkie friends with her, which made it very hard.

Beverly got on to heavy drugs. I should never have got Beverly involved in going on the game again. I really shouldn't have. You don't realise it at the time. I think she should have been there for her two children. They took her kids away because of the drugs. Whoever 'they' are—'social workers'—came and took them. They asked me if I would take Beverly's kids. I said, 'How can I? I'm just about to have a baby!'

Beverly's children were fostered out and then Beverly got picked up by the police for having drugs. She got put in Long Bay Gaol and I asked this businessman to pay bail for my sister to get out of jail. He agreed as long as she paid him back. Well, she didn't pay him back and he got the shits and I told him politely where to fuck off. Beverly got her kids back after a few years. She hasn't had an easy life.

Queensland

Once I had Michael, when I was 27, I stopped everything and came and lived up in Queensland with my sister Gloria and didn't go back on the game. I had the baby and my dad said, 'I'm going to take you up to your older sister in Maroochydore.' I got a place right on the beachfront.

Michael was still a baby and I was on the single mother's pension. The owners, instead of me paying rent, said, 'If you clean the units when people move out, we won't charge you any rent.' I was a good mother but not an excellent one. I used to go to the pub a lot. I wish I'd been a better mother.

Anyway, I'm in Maroochydore and dad says to me, 'Beverly's getting out of jail.' She had ended up going in again because all the time she was whacked out on drugs. We drove down to Silverwater, in Sydney, and got Beverly out and she came back up and stopped with me in my unit. The police kept nagging us all the time. The police came and raided my house. They would rip my place apart. I put a complaint in about them and I was just told that I had an ex-convict living with me. I said, 'But that's not me! Why do that to my home?'

I was fed up to the bloody neck with it. I was sick of it. So we moved to Caloundra. She had a unit and I had a unit. She was on the corner and I was back up a bit further. I was on the pension but I'd met somebody else who was helping me financially and my dad was there a lot, not that I was very fond of my father. Any man that doesn't come near his daughter until she's 18, I don't think's a father's bum hole. He was an old drunk.

We packed up and moved to Bulimba and I had a big fight with Beverly. She up and went to Sydney and I followed her not long afterwards. I was working at Royal Doulton making hand basins and earning good money too and Michael was at school. My life centred around my child. I was with a bloke but I never married him. I'm not that stupid. Men are only useful as sperm banks. I met him up the pub when I was living near Beverly. On a Friday or Saturday night she'd say, 'Do you want to go out? I'll mind Michael.' We got a house in Chatswood. He was offered a job as a supervisor in a garbage company in Brisbane and he asked me if he bought a house would I move up there with him? I didn't know if I wanted to go that far because I didn't really want to be associated with a bloke again. I didn't have much time for them. He said if I come up to Queensland that I will never have to work another day. Within a month I had three jobs—cleaning jobs. Prick, he was. When I first moved here he put me in a caravan and I used to cry every day and say I was moving back to Sydney. We moved into the house I'm in now on Michael's tenth birthday. But we still live in the same house and that's since 1978. That's a lot, a lot of years. That's worse than a death sentence.

I had a heart attack in 1985 through all the stress that this prick has put me under. I was only 40. He was playing up on me. If she had been anything to look at, I could understand but she was as ugly as a hatful of arses. Then he moved his mother in here and she used to shake up to me. She only come up to my shoulder and I'd say to her, 'Listen short arse, don't start with me cos I'll knock you into next week and your son will come next.' I told him, 'Either she goes or I go' and she went.

We live in the same house but we're not together anymore. In 2001, he hit me. We'd been drinking. The ambulance took me to hospital because my nose was spurting blood. The coppers took him away but they brought the bastard back. I had to go to court but I dropped the charges and he's never laid a hand on me since then. He knows better. I don't let any man put their hand on me. I say to them, 'Remember, you've always got to go to sleep!' He lives downstairs and I live upstairs. We talk but there's no intimate relationship. Michael thinks of him as his father. I made good money as a cleaner and getting other people to work with me. I was doing that until I was 69. Michael moved out three years ago and he's now 44. He was married but they split up. They've got a child. I get on all right with her and I dearly love my grandson.

Two years ago, I found out that I am Aboriginal. Gloria kept telling me and I said, 'Oh bullshit!' Then she sent me all the paperwork and I am now quite proud of the fact that I'm from one of the first owners of this land. Our grandmother, on my mother's side, was a native of New South Wales, a Kuringgai woman.

The Forde Inquiry and Aftermath

I started looking at my past when Leneen Forde opened the inquiry in 1998. I wrote a letter. I think Uniting Care were the first ones who came to us. I went back to Wolston Park to visit and they said, 'What are you doing here?' I said, 'Minding my own business. Why don't you try it sometime?' We were basically segregated from the Forde Inquiry. We went to one meeting where Peter Beattie announced compensation and they said that any women who went into Wolston Park were to go into another room.

By then I was starting to get really feisty and I said, 'Why are we being put in a separate room?' They told us that Wolston Park wasn't part of the Forde Inquiry. It seemed to be all done hushy-hushy.

There was one meeting in City Hall and they took me outside because I was going off my head. All the people who had been in institutions were sitting on the left-hand side and all the suits were sitting on the right-hand side. The women who had been in institutions were singing songs and I thought, 'How can you sing to these people as though nothing's happened?'

Beattie had a huge budget for this and I'm sure that some of this money went to pay for all these meetings with the suits—women dressed up to the nines with diamonds dripping off their hands. I think they were being paid to sit and listen to all the bullshit that they spoke. The people on the left looked like homeless people and I just thought about the difference between that side and the other side. They've got no idea what these people are going through and I just completely lost my temper.

The people from Lotus Place came and got me and took me outside and I had a cigarette and they said, 'Let's go back inside', and I said, 'No. I'm going home. I'm not putting up with this bullshit.' I started to become outspoken. My blood pressure was out of control during the Forde Inquiry. I did receive a payout from the Queensland Government but that wasn't for being in Wolston Park but for being in the other institutions. I think the worst ones of the lot of them as far as having a bit of heart is the Salvation Army. I think they were bloody disgraceful. I really do. I tell you what, didn't I give them what for, too! I hated the Salvation Army. I hate them with a deep, abiding passion because they came through my house. There was two of them came through and a third one wanted to come through and I told him to bugger off, 'No, you're not coming through my house. I have enough of youse.'

They rang up my brother Chris who I did not have contact with for 29 years, but who's now come back into my life. He rang up the Children's Commissioner, 'What you did to my sister was an out-and-out disgrace'. We get on like a house on fire. We're as mad as two cut snakes. He's two years younger than me. He's a wealthy man but I don't ask anything of him and I don't expect anything of him. Any money that I've been given, I've invested it. His wife doesn't like me because of what I used to do for a living.

Beverly passed away in 2009, when she was 67, of chronic renal failure and hepatitis C. I loved Beverly. On my mirror, I've got a photo of her when she was a baby. She and I were so close but Beverly never had the strength that I've got. I don't smoke or drink because of my hepatitis. I got it off Beverly.

I never had a proper education because we were Home children. The teachers weren't interested in us but I was always very good at English. Mathematics, I'm hopeless at. I've been an avid reader. I read anything. I've got newspapers everywhere on my bed. The fact that we were denied an education is an absolute disgrace because I could be sitting in a high-profile job. I blame the Uniting Church for that. They didn't think then that girls should go on.

Shithead Petersen didn't care.[1] As far as he was concerned we were juvenile delinquents. He never stopped to think that maybe we were fed up with being institutionalised. I'd been in institutions ever since I was one and a half. I say, 'What if it happened to you or one of your children?'

Wolston Park affected me really badly. I'm embarrassed to say that I was placed in Wolston Park mental hospital. Immediately you say that you've been placed in a mental hospital people think, 'Oh, she must be mental'. I'm far from bloody mental. I'm only a nut when I see the funny side of life. I've got a damned good sense of humour but I don't take shit from no bastard. These people taught me to hate. They taught me to be one of the most persistent bitches that you've ever come across in your bloody life.

I'm still up in counselling through the Salvation Army and she's helping me a lot. I must admit that. I'm a very angry person but I'm trying not to be because the only person the anger hurts is me. I'm a really strong woman. I'm not full of shit. I never have been and I never will be. I don't like people who lie and I don't like people who bullshit. What you see with me is what you get and if you don't like it—stiff. And I will do everything, everything in my power to get a public hearing in the Royal Commission, but they don't care about us, do they? If I was younger, I'd buy a Winnebago and bugger off on my own.

---

1   Joh Bjleke-Petersen was the premier of Queensland from 1968–87.

4

Wasted Days and Wasted Nights: Rose

In 1956, when I was four, my mother put me into this penguins' orphanage. That's the nuns. We called them 'the penguins'. Mum couldn't look after us. When my dad come home from war, things didn't go right for them. Dad was shot and also caught malaria in New Guinea and that affected him after the war. It done something to his thinking. He wasn't my dad. He went his way and mum went her way. Going back in them days, there was no money. We were poor. My mother couldn't afford to keep us. She couldn't look after us and so that's where we ended up—in Tufnell Home. The abuse I got from them bloody penguins if we didn't do our chores properly—like have the floor shining so you could see your face in it: we got the cane.

And there were smaller children there—too small to do any scrubbing—but the nuns would belt them. I stood in front of the little ones to cop it so they wouldn't get the cane for not doing their chores. Even though I was little myself, only four, I was bigger than the smaller ones—they were only two or three years old—and so I protected them. Once the nuns threw me in this bloody dark broom closet. It was pitch black. So I pushed one of the nuns and her glasses fell off. I laughed. She shut me in and said, 'Nothing will come of your life! You're the devil's daughter!'

They also used to make us wear these shoes that were too small and tight on our feet. I used to kick them off and walk with bare feet. I got caned for that and back in the broom closet I go. I was petrified because there was no light, no nothing. Even now I have to always have a light on and I have claustrophobia. They done that to me. Once, when I was nearly five, I was on the top of the slippery dip and one of the bigger kids pushed me off and I broke my arm. They took me to Brisbane Hospital and fixed my arm up in plaster. It was a bloody good weapon, that!

I didn't find out until then that Margaret was my sister. She was also in Tufnell. These two little kids, said, 'Hey Rosie! You know you got a sister in here?' I said, 'Huh? Where is she?' Margaret was standing right near the door. They said, 'That's your sister there—Margaret.' She was a year younger than me.

Then I got fostered out, with Margaret, to these morons who lived out in the country, out in Woop Woop. Being small we didn't know what was going on. We weren't told anything. My foster mother was an old crow. She was very strict. We had to empty out their piss pot and it had poop in it. This was our job every morning and also wipe everything down and pick up rubbish. There was no love. Nothing. Our foster mother made these ruddy old-fashioned hag dresses that I refused to wear. There was no way. They were old granny things, going back half a century before. I got mine and Margaret's dress and I ripped them up. I said, 'I'm not wearing it!'

We were sent to Benarkin School and, because I didn't understand the schoolwork, the bloody headmaster would give me the cane. I was nine years old. This went on day after day after day, in front of all the other children in class.

At home, the foster dad would take off his belt and whack us. One day, I went and got a razor and yelled to them, 'You dogs! You make us do this and do that! Watch out!'

I wasn't really going to cut myself. It was just a threat. I wasn't going to let them hurt Margaret. But I got sent back to Tufnell Home. I was 12. I didn't see Margaret again until 45 years later.

I kept running way from Tufnell Home. I'd run down to this old woman's place and hide under her house. She'd feed me and then she'd ring the nuns up to tell them where I was. The nuns called the cops. I hate cops. I was so terrified of them. I remember them grabbing my arm—one on each side. They took me back to Tufnell. But I kept running away.

At 13, I got picked up again by the police and they took me back to Tufnell again but the nuns didn't want me this time and so they arranged it with welfare to have me taken to Goodna mental hospital. Welfare people from the government came and got me. I hate the government. They had no right putting me in there. There was nothing wrong with my mind.

It was 1965 when the head of staff at Goodna put me up in Ward 8 with violent mental patients. They bashed me up. The staff would take me into this room and give me shock treatment. I was put in a straightjacket and also given all these medications. For breakfast, lunch and tea, they had us on these drugs. There was one—Paraldehyde. When I had it, I didn't know what bloody day it was or where I was. Everything was strange and frightening. It took a couple of days before I come back to be myself. There was this bloody doctor who would examine me all over. The nurses were nasty to me and the other girls. They also took me down this bloody hallway, into a room, on a bed and strapped my legs, strapped my arms and put something like a halo on each side of my temples and then they plugged it in. When I had this shock treatment, I could be out for days. My eyes would all roll all the bloody way back. I wouldn't know what day it was. Everything was just all gone. It fries your brain. My hair looked like barbed wire and there was no toothbrush to clean my teeth. I just wanted to get out of Goodna. I was petrified of violent patients and I thought I would die from the shock treatment and all the drugs.

Something went wrong with one of the shock treatments. I ended up in the Brisbane Hospital. Then I was returned to Goodna in a freer ward with other teenage girls. At least I didn't get bashed up but I was still given medication and shock treatment about once a week or once a fortnight. I told one of the nurses how much it all hurt. She said, 'You girls shouldn't even be in here.' She was nice. She stuck up for us kids but she had to be very careful. Some of the girls had their families come and see them. The gate was wide open in that ward and that was my chance to piss off. The cops picked me up for vagrancy. They asked my name. They said, 'Oh! We've been looking for you!'

They caught me and put me back in Goodna and I was there until I was 14. I ran away again and the bastards didn't get me this time. I never, ever went back. I hitchhiked to the town of Roma. There, I met a bunch of street kids and stayed with them for a few months, under the bridge and also in rubbish bins to keep warm. There was about a dozen of us aged from 10 to 18. Then it was time for me to move on. I wanted to be free as the breeze. I went with the wind. I hitchhiked to South Australia. I got picked up by truckies. I was petrified but I didn't know what I was going to do. They'd asked me where I'd like to be dropped off. I'd say, 'Just down here. I've got friends here.' I lied. I didn't have anyone. I'd keep heading off hoping to find a place where I'd be loved and looked after. I'd survive by taking food from garbage bins.

I ended up in a country town in South Australia by the beach. I met a new friend on the beach—Brenda. She was 14. I saw her mother once, sitting at the bus stop. She was Aboriginal. There were these little shacks at the beach. We'd hide in there and if we heard anyone, then we were off. Brenda and I stuck together. I could trust her with my life. I wasn't scared around her. We ended up in Sydney in Kings Cross. A truckie was going that way and he dropped us off there. He said someone there would come and help. We didn't know anything about Kings Cross just that there were more garbage bins for food and somewhere to hide.

We were standing on a corner at Kings Cross near the brothel bit. This woman came out to have a smoke and started asking us all these questions. She taught us how to get into prostitution. We used to call her 'Mother'. She was a nice person who looked after us but if you 'flipped the page over in the book', she was entirely different. She was nice but she was also mean. She taught us what do by showing us pictures. I didn't keep on doing what she wanted me to do. I did it for a while but something inside was telling me that it was the wrong thing. So she kicked me out and I had nowhere to stay. Brenda stayed on but I took off.

I had no money. I went wherever I could, wherever I felt safe—behind shops, in little humpies, garbage bins. I had a daughter—a rape baby. I don't know who her father is. I just don't know. Father unknown. I got raped on the streets. My stomach just kept on swelling. I had the baby in New South Wales. Karen was born with brain damage. Later, in the early 1980s, I took Karen to the specialist. I was telling him about some of my past. I asked him, 'Why was my daughter born like that? Was it all the medications that them bastards in Goodna was shoving into me?' He said, 'There is a good, possible chance because your daughter is not the only one. I've had so many children come to me who are crippled and other things.' I said, 'But getting back to me, you've read the medications they gave me—Paraldehyde and the other things.' He said, 'It's a good, possible, bloody chance.'

4. WASTED DAYS AND WASTED NIGHTS

Anyway, after Karen was born, we lived on the streets and I looked after her by going to different churches to get food and clothing. It was hard but we always slept where there were streetlights shining. I could at least see if there was someone sneaking around. Then I met a nice man, Carl, in the pub. He was 18. Karen was five. I went out with Carl for eight years. We came to Western Australia because Carl had friends over there. He had a job—a jack of all trades and helped look after Karen. I was a stay-at-home mum and bottle washer. Carl and I had two daughters of our own—Pipi and then Shannon. Pipi is a New Zealand name because Carl is a Kiwi. In 1978, when I was 27, he pissed off home to New Zealand. He wanted to marry his first cousin. It was very confusing for me. He's still with her to this day.

Then Carl didn't give me any money to look after the children. A woman took me to social security and I got money. They got me into one of their safe houses right out in the sticks. I didn't like it and they got us a place in Fremantle. Then I moved into a caravan park. That's where Pipi died in 1991 when she was 13. She suffered with bronchial asthma and she was on several tablets and the poison from those had built up in her system and killed her. It was on her death certificate. I still miss her. I'll never get over it. It's like there's a big piece taken out of my life. I still have all of her things with me. I've lived still loving her. If I feel sad I think of her, have a little cry and say, 'Pipi, I wish you were here.'

I moved to a farmhouse because Carl's brother come over for a holiday. I always kept in contact with Carl's mum. She's a very nice person and she lives in New South Wales. I moved from the farmhouse close to the city to be near doctors in case one of my children got sick. I was a mother, father, aunty, uncle and all to my children. I'm also a carer to Carl's brother. My daughter Karen is 45 now and Shannon is aged 40. As well as brain damaged, Karen is also an epileptic and she's been on a disability pension since she was 16 years of age. She lives in a unit as part of a complex not far from where I live. I help her with cooking and her housework. I love her to death but she's bloody hopeless! Shannon is married with five children and has got her own business—washing, cleaning and polishing cars. My eldest granddaughter has got two babies now.

I found my sister Margaret through social security. They got in contact with her to see if she wanted to get to know me. We got talking on the phone. Margaret came over here by plane and I met her at the airport. People from TV were there too. We were on TV and in the paper because we hadn't seen each other for 45 years. Margaret's not a rich person and it took time for her to save money to come to Perth. I was on top of the world when I saw Margaret. I couldn't believe it. I wanted to get on top of the highest roof and sing it out. I was just so happy. Margaret stayed with us. We shared the one bed! Margaret stayed for about a week and a half and then she had to get back to her husband and her family. I didn't want Margaret to go back. We haven't seen one another since. We talk on the phone.

Them welfare mongrels took my whole life from me. When I was a little girl, I always wanted to be in the army. Always. Even when I grew up and was doing other things, I still wanted to be in the army. But I wasn't fit to be in the army. I've had no education. That was a dream of mine—be in the army, own my own home, money in the bank. Nup. It didn't happen because bloody Goodna and the bloody welfare mob and the politician dorks took my life, took my dream.

I've got no recall of years of my life. I just can't remember. And when I speak up about my childhood I talk the way I did when I was a child. Also I don't want to go down that path of things that happened after I came out of Goodna and long before I met Carl. I don't talk about that because I still suffer from deep depression. But there's also bits and pieces missing that I don't know anything about. That has to be from the shock treatment because I wasn't into drugs or anything like so what else could it have been? There was nothing wrong with my brain before they gave me all the shock treatments and drugs. Wasn't then but now there's a lot of things I just can't remember. Margaret did all the talking for me with the commission because it's too depressing for me. I've never applied for redress. I don't understand it.

Carl's brother is 50. He's disabled with hip problems and he's an alcoholic. I get paid for caring for him. They call it 'live-in carer'. We live in a two-bedroom duplex in a housing estate. We rent it off Homes West that helps people with disabilities. He's got his room and I've got mine. When he's pissing me off I go and tell him, 'Go and piss off to the back yard.'

Margaret and I have uncles and half-sisters who don't want nothing to bloody do with us. They're married into rich families. Margaret and I aren't good enough to be related to them. They've got everything. Margaret and I have bloody nothing. It gets to me these days. Family is supposed to stick together. That's what I always believe. I find it very hard to trust anybody. I don't mix with other people. I keep to myself. There's things I like doing like dancing but I don't go out anywhere. I'm at home here and I do my own thing. That's my whole bloody life—just gone right to the shit. At times it's hard but I've managed and I've done everything all my life. I haven't asked anyone for anything. I just do what I've got to do. I go to my room to talk to my daughters on the phone and I play country music. My favourite song is 'Wasted Days and Wasted Nights' by Freddy Fender.

Even though I live in the poor house, I'm a good person and I'd do anything for anyone. That's all I can do. I reckon between the bloody welfare mob and the bloody government, they oughta buy me a bloody house so I can have my daughter Karen live with me. It would be heavenly. I reckon they owe that to me.

5

Don't Shoot the Wounded: Tammy

Stolen

My Aboriginal mum was one of the Barkanji people, from Wilcannia in New South Wales. I understood that she used to travel to and from Cunnamulla in Queensland to Bourke in New South Wales. She got pregnant in Cunnamulla from a shearer named Billy. I was her first daughter, born in 1960. My mum was living in a place on the banks of the Warrego River. When I was three months old, the white police came and she hid from them behind a bush because she had had polio and couldn't run very fast. When the time came to go, she accidentally dropped me in the river. She couldn't swim and so she couldn't save me. The white police got me and took me to the government-run Diamantina Children's Home.

Adopted

The staff at the Home didn't let my adoptive mum take me home at first because I was very sick and they thought I was going to die. But I got better and I grew up with my adoptive mum and dad in Brisbane. Dad was a tram driver. They were really good to me. We'd go on holidays. One year, they took me to sing Carols by Candlelight in Sydney and I got up on stage and sang with Barry Crocker. One year, they took me to Melbourne and we went on the rides on top of the Myers building. They let me see the movies *Born Free* and *The Sound of Music* twice because

I liked them so much. They really loved me. We had a Pomeranian dog named Kym and a cat named Timothy. Mum also had a pet bird named Harry that would never shut up!

So I was a healthy and happy, innocent child that saw everybody in the world as being good and nice. I was brought up by a good Christian mum and dad who used to take me to Sunday school. I used to sit on a swing and sing while I swung up and down but I used to rock myself. I didn't see things the way other kids did. I used to do some strange things. When I was three I got on a piano and played up and down the keyboard, which I never, ever learned or played before. I would create things. I made buildings from plates and saucers and cups. When I was four, I was diagnosed with autism. When I was five, my mum didn't know if I would be able to go to a normal school so she took me to a psychiatrist and he would come to visit me at home and sit on the floor and watch me play. I was then sent to a neurologist who told mum that I had savant syndrome, which meant that he thought that I could cope with normal school, but they didn't know that I had dyslexia. That, together with autism, made school a lot worse. The smartness in me was the worst thing that I ever had because I knew I could do things but in different ways to everybody else and no one understood. I was frustrated and angry. I also used to wear these stupid shoes with callipers to stop me walking inwards. The other kids used to hit me and make fun of me. I used to look out the window at the birds because they had freedom. They didn't know about dyslexia at my school and so they just thought that I was a problem child. I used to get the 'cuts' all the time for not answering the right questions and for not doing my schoolwork. I hated going to school. It was terrible. I ran away from school to go home. Why should I go to school to get hurt? That's bullshit.

When I was six, a kid at school was making fun of me for being adopted. I didn't know what she was talking about. She lived in our street and my adoptive mum knew her mum who was called 'Courier Mail' because she had the biggest mouth in the street.

So I asked my mum and she told me, 'Mummy and Daddy couldn't have any children so we went and got you.' When I was seven, Kym the dog died, my grandmother died and my dad had stomach cancer. I remember visiting him in hospital and he told me that I had to help mum. He died. He was 52 years old. Mum had a breakdown and went into hospital. My aunties wouldn't look after me and I was put into Sandgate Home for a couple of months. It was terrible there. I didn't want to talk or play with the other kids. When mum got out of hospital, she came and took me out of there. She didn't know what was wrong with me because I wasn't talking. She took me to a doctor who said that I was suffering from shock. Mum sent me back to school. The kids called me 'retard' and bashed me up and so I kept running away from school.

Wilson Youth Hospital

I was picked up by the police and sent to the Winston Noble Unit, a mental health ward in the Prince Charles Hospital, Chermside, Brisbane. I was seven. I remember the nurses saying that I shouldn't be there and they used to piggyback me around the grounds. That was great fun but I ran away because I wanted to be home with mum. That's all my crime was—running away from these places to go home to where I was loved. Then I was sent to Lowson House, then back to Chermside, then back to Lowson House. When I was 11, I was sent to Wilson Youth Hospital. It had three sections—Treatment, Remand and Privilege. I didn't like it because they drugged me up all the time. They gave me this green syrup that used to knock me out and also make me hallucinate. It was Melleril. I was on Largactil too. I used to fall asleep at the table with the other kids but they wouldn't let me sleep and they tried sitting me up all the time. I got nasty and grumpy with them and so I was kept in seclusion in a lock-up room. I practically lived there. They had to take me on 'dog' walks—it was a little corridor where I would walk up and down with the nurse and then they would put me back in seclusion. I was sexually abused by some of the staff because I was on my own, away from all the other kids. I was so doped up that they could do whatever they wanted.

After nine months, I was sent home to my mum because a doctor at Wilson said I should never have been sent there. But when I got home, I had bad dreams all the time about the nurses touching me up. I didn't know what to do. Also, mum had to work all the time. Mum took me to a doctor who suggested that I only needed to put under observation for a little while but another doctor who was higher up, and didn't even see me, sent me to an adult hospital. I wanted to go home and they wouldn't let me, as usual, so I ran away and went home. Mum made me go to another doctor and so I went and knocked on the door of Wilson Youth Hospital because I didn't want to go to another adult institution but Wilson wouldn't let me in. So I ran away and the police took me back to

Wilson. I was treated as an uncontrollable child. I remember the priest in there.[1] He was on our side. I think it was shocking what they did to him. They sacked him. I reckon that when someone sticks up for us, they should listen. All they could do was tell him that he had to go. I reckon that was wrong.

Wolston Park

I was 13 when I was sent to Wolston Park from Wilson Youth Hospital. They just said that I had to be moved on because I was getting older. The first day I got out of the car at Wolston Park, the head doctor was standing outside Osler House, smoking his pipe and said to me, 'If I put you into an open ward, will you stay here or run away and go home to your mother?' All I did was shrug my shoulders and for that I was put into Osler House.

A couple of years later they tried me in Noble House, an open ward for two weeks but I was sent back to Osler House. Being there nearly killed me and it's a wonder I'm still standing.

Figure 3: Noble House, Wolston Park Hospital Complex, 2004.
Source: Photograph courtesy of the Department of Environment and Science, Queensland Government.

---

1   The personal history of the priest mentioned here is the subject of Chapter 6 in this book.

At six o'clock in the morning, they got me up and made me have a shower. If I was feeling tired because of the medication, they would drag me to the shower, and if I protested they would kick me. If I got a nice nurse, I would just have cold water poured on me. Male nurses would stand and watch me shower. That was wrong. They got great enjoyment out of that. Then we had to line up for our tablets and then we would have breakfast. Then they'd just chuck us outside in the yard that was fenced off. Then we'd have tea and then we were locked in our cells at 8 o'clock at night. The staff would play cards. They were getting paid for doing nothing.

Every night we were locked up in separate, isolated cells with a bucket. I'd be waiting for someone to come in and rape and bash me. Every night I was thinking, 'Is tonight the night that I'm gonna die?' I would feel the shame and feel numb and there was nothing I could do about it. My insides felt dirty. I was just a kid. In the showers at night I was also sexually assaulted. It depended on which staff were on. The nurse Joseph was the ringleader. He would bring others into the ward. These guys were sickos. In the hallways, you could hear screaming. There was other young girls in Osler House. We were too scared to tell each other what they did to us. I could smell the urine and vomit. I was drugged up all the time but I had to try to stay awake to protect myself from being attacked by a patient or by staff. I was on Melleril, Stelazine, Largactil, Cogentin and Lithium. I was also on Serapax and Serenace but I was allergic to them and so they had to give me other drugs like Artane to treat the bad side effects. Plus, at night I was on a barbiturate tablet called 'Phenobarb' and was also given a Modecate injection once a month. My god! They all got away with it. Everything was so covered up. If I reported being raped I was told that I was mad. I didn't get pregnant because I was given the Depo Provera contraceptive injection. The good nurses were too scared to tell anyone what was going on.

We hardly saw the Patient's Friend. If we spoke out I would be stripped naked and given a Paraldehyde injection. So what the hell was she there for if we weren't allowed to speak to her? We were wards of the state and the state was supposed to look after us. Child safety and mental health really fucked up. A judge used to come to Osler House once a month to see if there was anything wrong with the place and to see if anything was needed. The hospital would get a call from head office saying that the judge was coming. There were no toilets in the cells. When the judge was going to come, we had to clean out our buckets and then they'd be put away. So the judge wouldn't have known that we only had buckets for a toilet. Did the judge write any reports? Are these on file? Some staff would make fun of me—bringing up my past. I was stripped off naked. I have scars on my arms today from being made to have blood tests every fortnight. I was also a self-mutilator because I had to keep my sanity. When I was raped or hurt too much I would cut myself because pain-plus-pain relieves pain. It would also stop me from hurting other people. That was my life for eight years until I was 21—being treated like a dog in a cage.

Mum came and visited me at Osler House three times a week. She would get on a bus, then she'd catch a train and then walk three quarters of a mile to Wolston Park and then all that to get home again. She did all that because she loved me. On some visits, she'd arrive at Osler House and they wouldn't let her see me. Wolston Park broke her heart. She tried to get me out. She went and saw the head of child safety. She went and saw solicitors. They told her that I needed to be there because if I got out, I would be a danger to myself. That wasn't true. Mum wanted me to come home. She understood what I was going through. I stayed alive hoping she would get me out.

Escape

A new nurse arrived at Osler House in 1980. She was young and she didn't like what they were doing to me. She got into trouble for talking to me. After she had been working there for six months, she said that she would let me out and to go and hide in the church. She said that when she finished her shift, she would pick me up and take me home to my mum. She unlocked the door and I bolted. I hid in the church and waited for hours—all afternoon. The nurse came and drove me home. My mum jumped in the nurse's car and we drove together to Lady Cilento's house. My mum had got in touch with Lady Cilento, trying to get her to do something to get me out. She was a well-known doctor and wrote in the *Courier Mail* and started child centres. She was really important. Her husband was a doctor, too, and years before had been the director-general of health and medical services.

Lady Cilento saw me and said, 'My god! My darling! What are they doing to you? They are killing you with all these drugs.' I could hardly stand up. She got on the phone straight away and rang Wolston Park and said that they had to make sure that I would stay out of the place or she would expose what was going on. I was really doped up but I still thought it was great that someone cared enough to do something. I saw her at her place a couple of times after that. She weaned me off the drugs with vitamins.

On the Streets and Parenthood

I had complex post-traumatic stress disorder. I would get up after a bad dream and if I didn't plant my feet firmly on the ground, I would get a flashback. I heard patients in Wolston Park screaming. I couldn't breathe properly. I felt hot. I got scared. I didn't know what to do. I was going off my head. There were times when neighbours rang the police. So I left home because I didn't want to hurt my mum. Those mongrels at Wolston Park made a real bad bastard out of me. I was an adult but I hadn't been allowed to grow up properly. They had stopped me from growing up with my mother's love. It was like being locked up again but on the outside. I was locked up with anger and revenge—locked up with hurt. I didn't know what to do with myself. I lived on the streets—under the Queen Street bridge. Sometimes I'd end up in the hospital because I was cutting myself. The only people who would take me for who I was were alcoholics and junkies. I had to stop people screaming in my head. I had to stop going back into that old place.

On 10 December 1982, I had a baby who I called 'Darren' with one of the guys I used to drink with on the street. I was really fond of that guy. His name was Graham but my mother didn't like him and she and I used to fight about him. Graham was more sensible than me. He had a job and a flat. Graham took care of Darren and he treated me nice. Darren was just like me and he was smart. But when he was five he got really sick. We found out he had leukaemia. We took him to hospital for transfusions and other treatments. I really hate the 31st of December every year, because that's when Darren got really sick. He died at 1:30 am on New Year's Day. Darren's death really upset Graham and he and I split up after that. If Darren had lived, I probably would have made a go of it with his father. I dream about all the possibilities of doing so many things with Darren. I miss him.

Then I had a dog that lived with me under the bridge. Once, he kept lying with his head on my stomach and pawing at me. I went to the doctor who told me I was pregnant. The dog had known. I didn't know who the father of this baby was. Sometimes I shot up too much drugs and anyone could take advantage of me. I hated myself for that but it was the only thing that helped my PTSD. I found a place—a squat—and I rounded up all my friends on the street and got them to tie me to the bed to get me off drugs. I went through my own cold turkey. I kicked the habit. I could fuck my own life up but I couldn't fuck up a kid's life. I was 24. I started going home and asking my mum for help. The doctors were saying that the baby would have to be taken off me that I would never be able to look after it because I was Tammy-the-druggie, Tammy-the-alcoholic who couldn't read, who couldn't add up, who couldn't do anything. I was like a wounded cripple that no one could do anything with. I told my mum that I wanted my baby to be adopted into a nice family but there was a nurse in the Mater Hospital who told me that she never gave up on me and supported me through the whole pregnancy.

Another woman also taught me how to write. Before then all my writing was back-to-front. My 'ds' were 'bs'. My 'ys' were 'hs'. It was pathetic, actually. I couldn't see the letters properly. Then it got really easy for once. I learned that a 'u' was a toilet bowl. A 't' was a cross. I identified the things that I see every day with the alphabet. I just needed to get a picture in my head to get the letters right. Also, when I lived on the streets in the city, I sometimes used to go to the Coles cafeteria in town to get a coffee and I got to know this doctor who had his surgery upstairs in the same building. He spent time with me because he actually thought that I had brains and that I was the worst case of institutional abuse that he had ever seen. When he didn't have appointments, he taught me how to use a computer. He was decent. Once I learned, I was with it. That all helped to start the new Tammy.

Rachel

I had a caesarean and gave birth to Rachel in 1984. I left the hospital but Rachel stayed behind. She was a sick, premmie kid. Then something inside me made me run up the steps with all the stitches in me, I didn't give a shit, to where Rachel was on the top floor. And there she was. She put her little arms up to me. I really loved Rachel. I would visit and bath her and I took her home. But then the medical people 'ripped my guts out' because of my past. I took her to the Royal Brisbane Hospital for check-ups and they said that I was forgetting to feed her. Whatever she ate she wasn't putting on weight. They were trying to get my daughter off me. I took her to the hospital when she got sunburnt. But I made a mistake—I was living with this group of no-hopers at Boreen Point at the beach and I didn't know about the rays of the sun. I took her to the hospital because she was crying. I did that three times. Next minute, they took her off me. Lunatic-me left her there at the hospital. When I came home without my daughter, my mum yelled at me. She told me that I gave them what they had wanted from day one. I went back to the hospital to get my kid back and they wouldn't let me see her. They got security staff. They told me that they had put an order on me so I couldn't visit my daughter. What could I do? I started drinking again. I had done everything that I was told to do. I fed her. I clothed her. They couldn't prove that I wasn't feeding her. I will not take the rap that I ever starved her. She was a hypertonic baby. Only recently I was told that she's lacking some muscles in her body. That's why she was underweight.

Anyway, one of the teams at the hospital said that I should be allowed to have a fair go and so one Christmas, an officer from child safety came and visited and said, 'Merry Christmas Tammy, I've brought Rachel home to be with you.' She was almost one. When Rachel was four, I took her to the hospital for a check-up. The night before I took her rollerskating. I always used to do that to get her muscles going. She liked it. We had so much fun and it would help her with her balance. I would also take her swimming. The water would support her. I knew what I was doing but the doctor laughed at me when I told him.

He said, 'If we don't do something about your daughter, she is going to die.' What sort of mother would I have been if I didn't let them keep her in hospital and look after her? I swear, I would do anything for her but they had no reason. This is what Wolston Park had done to me. The day they took her off me, I had to tell my four-year-old, 'I'm not allowed to come and visit you.' She said, 'Don't go Mummy.' I said, 'I have to go.' I gave her a kiss. She said, 'Don't go. It's important. You have to stay here.' I never heard her use the word 'important' before then. I didn't even think that she knew what 'important' meant.

I was so mad that one day I went to the Fortitude Valley Child Health Centre with two knives. I wasn't going to hurt anyone. I just wanted my daughter back. All these cop cars came. Oh boy—I was in trouble! I ended up in Rosemount Psychiatric Hospital. The head doctor at Rosemount had been my doctor at Wolston Park and had tried to get me out of Osler House. My stay at Rosemount was only supposed to be for 24 hours but

I stayed longer because they were helping me. He said he would help me get my daughter back. They rang and rang the Royal Brisbane Hospital where Rachel was. No one had the guts to tell us the real truth. Finally, they told me that they had taken her to foster parents. They had promised me a last visit. They didn't keep their promise. I went stupid. The doctors had to drug me. When I left Rosemount, I went back to the streets. Mum was wild with me. She couldn't believe that I was that stupid to give Rachel to the hospital.

Rachel's foster parents got to know me and told me, 'Child welfare should just see how you and Rachel get on together.' But it's never about how you get on with your child. It's about how you get on with the staff at child welfare and once you have a past, you always have a past. That's wrong. Why don't they give us back our files? My files are my life made into lies and that's what they look to judge how I am today. I was judged by my anger. I am not judged for who I really am. If I could go back, I would have just shut up and bit my tongue. Years later, they found out it wasn't my fault. I *had* fed Rachel properly but I am scarred for life because Rachel and I never got to know each other. We don't get on because we are two different people now. It's like my Aboriginal family—my brothers and sisters—we don't know each other the same way that we would have if we had grown up together. I think I came out pretty good given that I spent seven years in Wolston Park getting bashed and raped.

A social worker once said to me, 'You're nothing like how you're described in your files.' You see? I'm not a monster.

Work

After they took Rachel off me, I left Rosemount and went back to the streets. I tried to get my act together. I stopped shooting up. I tried to work out who 'Tammy' really was. I needed to create a 'Tammy' that I and other people would like—a 'Tammy' of brilliance, a good-natured 'Tammy'. I worked out how to get my own place. I needed to get a job. Even though a woman had helped me with my reading when I was pregnant with Rachel, it was only words. I couldn't comprehend big stuff. So I had to think what jobs I could do. I started selling the *Telegraph* newspaper on the streets. Then I got jobs at rides at the show grounds.

Some woman from the TAFE who knew me when I was on the streets reckoned I could learn and said, 'Be there every morning'. She was talking about Yeronga TAFE. So I went and learned how to read on computers. I learned about 'what comes next'. I learned how to write 'firstly', 'secondly' and 'in conclusion'. People got to know me—not people from the system, like social workers—but normal people and they would talk to me and give me ideas.

I thought about starting my own business. I saved up for my first industrial washing machine. Then I got my first industrial dryer. When I got three of each, I rented a place at the Gold Cost and got my laundromat going. Someone I knew taught me how to screen print and so I made my own T-shirts and got a stall selling them at the markets at the Gold Coast and the Sunshine Cost as well. Then I got contracts to make T-shirts for different organisations. I was earning good bucks. I opened another laundromat. I had two running and I was starting to feel that I was in control and doing something that could earn me money. Now I needed to look the part and I learned how to dress up like all the people who used to walk past me when I had been living on streets.

But because I could never get over losing Rachel and they said that I could never get her back, I went a bit crazy and ended up drinking and shooting up again and going back to the streets. I tried so hard to get Rachel back. I tried taking my own life a couple of times. I knew my child was special to me in many ways—the same way I thought of my adoptive mum.

Finding Mother

There were times when I wondered what my real mother was really like. When I was about 30 years old I wanted to know my real mum. My adoptive mum and I would fight about seeing my real mum because she didn't want me to get hurt. I wanted to find my real mum. I did my own detective work. I couldn't find her because she had got married and changed her last name. So I went to Cunnamulla to find her, where I was born. I started at the Aboriginal Co-op there and that search led me to the town of Bourke where the local Aboriginal community knew of my mum. I found out that she was living in Victoria then and I rang her up. When I met her she was so excited. I stayed with her for a couple of weeks with my other brothers and sisters. They accepted me. I felt great because I found my family. I pushed mum to tell me how I ended up being adopted. She told me that she couldn't read and so she signed my birth certificate with an X. She told me about how the police came. She told me that she was sorry that she couldn't run fast enough and that she couldn't swim and that she dropped me. Later she had rung Diamantina Home to find out where I was because she wanted me back. They told her that I was in a loving home.

Captive

I also found out that one of my brothers was in jail in the town of Sale in Victoria and I travelled to visit him. On my way to Sale, I passed through Mirboo North. I needed somewhere to stay and asked at St Vinnie's for help with accommodation. They told me about this refuge. It was a safe house run by a guy, Dave, who used to be a Salvation Army officer. I rang the place and Dave came and picked me up. He was nice and he took me to the jail at Sale to meet my brother. But then Dave wouldn't let me do anything without him. He drank a lot. He told me that he had been in jail. I wanted to leave the house. He wouldn't let me. He locked me in. He had the keys and a gun. I couldn't move. Another woman in the house, Stephanie, who was blind, had keys too. She'd do whatever he said. Dave raped and bashed me. He was a criminal. He had it all worked out. He'd go to St Vinnie's, and all these places, saying that he ran a safe place for women. He'd get the down-and-outers who didn't know better and then lock them up and do what he wanted. This is what Wolston Park did to me—left me dumb and vulnerable.

I tried to escape by ringing an ambulance and they took me to the hospital in Traralgon. I told the doctor what Dave was doing and he didn't believe me. He thought it was too far-fetched and so he admitted me to the psychiatric unit! Dave came to the hospital to pick me up wearing his old Salvation Army officer suit, making everyone think that he was a hero. He told the hospital staff that it was all in my head and that I made everything up. The only way the staff would let me out of the hospital was if I told them that everything I had said about Dave was a lie. That was the only way they were going to let me out! No one believed me. He was the man in the uniform. He had the credibility. They believed him before they even listened to me. The hospital returned me into the hands of this criminal. I was back in prison at Dave's house.

Another Escape

Dave used to supervise my phone calls. He made me ask mum on the phone to send down all my furniture and belongings from Brisbane, including my piano keyboard—things that I would never have moved. Mum knew something was wrong. My mum had to come down from Brisbane to save me. She came and stayed at the 'refuge' with me. I told Stephanie to do the right thing—get the keys and let us out. She did. I was finally free. I had been locked up there for two years and left pregnant because he had raped me. I took his gun to protect us in case he came after us. We went to the police. They didn't believe me. They said it was all my head. Mum went back to Brisbane. I wanted to stay and get my stuff back but that didn't work.

Anyway, I got the bus back to Brisbane and I got thrown off the bus, in town near Griffith, New South Wales, because I was sick. I had nowhere to go and so I went to a church. I started getting flashbacks. It was all so hopeless. I shut my eyes, said the Lord's Prayer, pointed the gun at my chest and fired. It missed my heart. Blood came out of my mouth. The one thing that kept going through my brain while I was lying there bleeding was what my mum would tell me, 'There is a lot of goodness in you Tammy, if you would just see that.'

The church neighbours heard the gun shot and rang the minister of the church. He found me and called for help. I ended up staying with the minister until I got better. He fed me and everything. He got the doctor to visit me every day and it was like living in a hospital with everything that was needed to treat me. He was a real friend. It took several months until I was better. I then got a bus to go home to Brisbane.

David

I rented a place to get ready for the baby. I wanted it to work this time. I knew that I could look after a baby. I wanted a boy. David was born in 1996 at Redcliffe Hospital. I named him after my adoptive father. All hell broke loose because when I had the caesarean, they accidentally put holes in my bowel. I needed surgery and was in intensive care and I couldn't see my baby. In the end they got me a room in the maternity ward and so I recovered in there. I had two colostomy bags. For weeks, I would hear all the different women having their babies.

Some would be calm and say, 'I'm trying to do the breathing. I'm breathing. I'm breathing.' Others would scream, 'HELP! FUCKING HELL!' It was interesting—ha! Better than TV!

Then they let me go home with David. I showed them that I was a good mum and that I didn't starve my kids. They got me the blue OzCare— St Vinnie's nurses who used to come around. But no one knew that David had an arachnoid cyst on the top layer of his brain. I reckon they nicked his head during the caesarean when they put holes in my bowel. But they didn't believe me when I said that he wasn't behaving like a normal kid. Later, on our way home from another visit with my Aboriginal mum in Victoria, we stopped off at the town of Parkes in New South Wales. I took David to the hospital because something wasn't right. He wasn't behaving like a normal baby. At that time, in the media, there were all these reports about family child abuse. As soon as they saw me and David, the hospital rang community services and accused me of bashing David. That made me wild and of course I started mouthing off but I was hurt. I knew I was innocent. New South Wales child safety services were brought in and they took David off me. I slept in my car, in Parkes, waiting to get my son back. They sent him off for a CAT scan and that's when they found out he had a cyst so they knew I hadn't hit him. I rang the child safety people at Redcliffe in Queensland because they knew me. I couldn't believe it. They were wonderful. They organised David to be taken back to Queensland and to be returned to me. I drove back to Brisbane and the Redcliffe child safety office brought David to me when I got home.

In 1999, my adoptive mum was in hospital because she had a stroke. She was in her eighties. I wanted to take her home and look after her but they told me that she was paralysed down one side. She couldn't talk. Then they didn't expect her to live through the night. I got on the bed and I told her that she couldn't go anywhere—she needed to stay with me a bit longer. I told her that there'd be no one to ring if I got sick. I had no real friends. I just had her. She died. They let me sleep there for the night. She went cold but she was my mum. I organised the whole funeral. Everyone who came reckoned that my mum would have been proud of me that day.

When my adoptive mum was in hospital, Dave, who kept me locked up in his house at Mirboo North, got caught. Two of the women from his house had called out for help when he took them shopping. Those women told the police everything that I had been trying to tell them three years ago. The police flew up to Brisbane and asked me to testify in court but my mum was dying and so I wouldn't help them, Besides, they didn't believe me the first time. Why should I help the cops? They didn't help me get away from him. Anyway, Dave ended up in Pentridge Prison.

David started at a school near Redcliffe. Some of the mothers volunteered to help the children in the classroom. One day, one of the mothers didn't turn up. Because I knew about computers the teacher asked me to help but the grade ones were not allowed to go to the library where the computers were. I thought, 'What bullshit!' So one day I led them to the library and I sat them down.

The teacher told them to call me 'Miss—whatever' but I said, 'No. Call me Tammy.'

I was really good with the kids. The school got me a government blue card so that I could work with children. At the school library, I made and photocopied computer workbooks for the children in grade one. The teacher was very impressed. My dyslexia made me a good teacher because I have had to learn how to break things up. I play a piano keyboard in a different way. I do it in dimensions that I make up—all minor chords are hit one, miss one, hit one, miss one and hit one. For example, it's C, F, G, A minor, D minor. I also crochet with the number eight. I count eight. You pull the thread around is 'one', you pull it through the hole is 'two' and so on. Every step has a number and that's why I can't get it wrong.

Now when it comes to computers, it's really easy. Inside the computer is the central processing unit but a child would never understand that. So what you do is call it 'the brain'. So I got the kids thinking about how their brain works. I got these grade one children learning how to save what they typed, to create their own files and to print. Some of the bloody mothers that got to help out at the school got jealous of me at one stage because my school shirt didn't have 'volunteer' on it. I had the same shirt that the teachers wore. That made me feel terrific. At the end of the year we invited the parents to a presentation where each kid explained something about the computer, 'This is what a mouse does', 'This is what a monitor does' and we sang songs in between—songs that I wrote.

But David wanted to live where there were more animals and I would do anything for him. So in 2002 we moved to the outskirts of Kingaroy. I lived for my son because I had nothing. He went to the local state school and the other kids bashed him up. The policeman told me that if he couldn't be safe at school, then take him out. So when he was in grade four, I took David out of school and did home schooling. All the home school materials cost an arm and a leg. Also, I was having problems with it because I didn't know how to do all that bloody work. It was beyond me. It got harder and harder every year. So I was stuck with a child I couldn't teach properly. This was different from helping kids at the school. I knew about computers but I didn't know all the things I had to teach David. In the end, I taught him the wrong ways so that he would get on in life. I taught him how to cheat. That's all I could do at the time. So I ended up with a child who spent his time on computers instead of doing his schoolwork and all hell broke loose. I got angry with him and it made my complex post-traumatic stress disorder worse. We were arguing all the time. I didn't know what to do.

I couldn't help David so I went to child safety but I didn't want them to take my son from me so I said that I was asking for a friend who needed help with home schooling. They said that that child would have to go to a foster family that could teach him properly. I freaked out when they said that. They'd rather take a child off a mother rather than giving her a chance. That's wrong. That's too much 'take your child off ya!' That's too much 'Your past is your past'. And really, none of us girls should have been locked up in Wolston Park the first place and so our past is not our bloody past. It wasn't our fault. We didn't do anything wrong.

I couldn't help David. I didn't want him to get bashed up at school and I didn't want child safety to take him off me and so David left home when he was 13 to live with his half-sister Rachel in Mackay. She put him into school and he got in the wrong company. David's friend there was mixed up in everything and knew how to play the system. He introduced David to a lot of bad things but he stood up for David and so no one hurt him.

Canberra

I hit the road. I was lost without my son. The person I was staying alive for was gone. I took two overdoses. I ended up in hospital in Canberra. I used to visit the National Library because it was free and there I found out about the history projects about Forgotten Australians including the exhibition at the National Museum. The politicians made it happen and I reckon they made themselves look good by doing that but at least it got survivors to be able to say what happened and someone took notice of us for once. All our lives no one believed us. We were just seen as idiots.

In Canberra I met people who cared, including a doctor who convinced me to go back to Queensland. She wrote a letter to David explaining to him about my post-traumatic stress disorder and how I really loved him. I went home and David came home too and brought his friend from Mackay. That didn't work too well. David fought with me. David ended up staying in residential care. It was his choice. He went back to live with Rachel. It took two years before David told me that I was right about his friend in Mackay. He came home and his exact words to me were, 'I know now that you were trying to protect me.'

Return to Brisbane

Others who were institutionalised have kids like mine. When David gets mad he says things to me like, 'You should have got me another mother' or 'You're fucked up with no brains' or 'You're a retard' or 'It's your fault for not getting me proper schooling!' I live with this today. The system was never there to help me. The system just fucked me over, putting it nice and bluntly. I didn't stand a chance. We should have got counselling. We shouldn't have had to do everything on our own. David is 20 now and still living with me. He had a couple of sessions with a counsellor that helped him deal with his emotional stuff with me, and he is now studying Year 10 at TAFE so that eventually he can finish Year 12. And I am proud of him and Rachel because they still call me 'mum' and they still love and care about me in their own ways. David also thinks I'm a good person because I help others in need. So maybe time will heal. I wish I was normal.

In 2012, I was at the local free breakfast for R U OK? Day. A guy that works in mental health was telling me to 'get on with my life'. He got me at crying point. The then head of a Catholic social service organisation, who I knew, said I could make a difference. I thought, 'What the bloody hell would she know!' I went roaring off to the local newspaper. There was a new journalist there who did a story on me and the opening lines were 'If Tammy had a dollar for every time she was told to "get on with her life", she would be rich'.

I was still angry about the conversation at the R U OK? breakfast so that when I slept I had these strong dreams. The first dream was me on a treadmill going nowhere. The second dream was my working in a morgue with the dead yelling for help but it was too late—they were already dead. The third dream was me back in Osler House and a voice said, 'You're still alive.' The fourth dream was my building the ark and all the animals helping me. The next dream was me running a drop-in centre.

Drop-In Centre

The next morning, I decided to make that dream come true. I would start a drop-in centre because there was nowhere for me to ever go when I needed it and so I thought that I would create the thing that had been missing in my life. I started ringing people up—individuals who helped me when the system didn't. Together we rent the church hall and run a drop-in centre from nine in the morning until 9:30 at night every Monday. Anywhere between 45 and 65 people come and everybody helps each other. We have a cook there and we serve meals to the homeless. Mothers come and bring their children. We teach people how to budget. I spend hours with these people. I get to know them. I get to know what they like. I am their friend. Local police and hospital staff refer homeless people in the area to me. When they phone me, I ring around and ask people I know if they would give someone a bed for the night. Sometimes, I sleep over with them to help. Sometimes I ring organisations and say I need money to put a homeless person in a motel for the night. Sometimes I drive the person-in-need for several hours to get to the nearest homeless shelter. There's a lot of people in my area who help me because they know I am really trying to make a difference.

This world is in a bad place—the greed—how can people get better if the government can't get a system right? There needs to be understanding of what it's like to be hurt instead of people staying away from us. There needs to be more emergency accommodation, support for parents-in-need instead of taking their kids off them—find out what their needs are—practical stuff. I have worked my arse off and I now have a Certificate III in micro business operations, a Certificate IV in training and assessment, Certificate II in IT and have completed the first six units in frontline management. I also have certificates in senior first aid and food handling and safety. At the moment, I'm doing an online diploma in mental health studies. Next, I'm going to do a course in being a facilitator in mental illness recovery and a Certificate IV in peer support training. In 2013, I graduated from the federally funded Leader for Tomorrow program. I've bettered my maths and English. I've trained in public speaking. I went to weekend workshops using music computer software because I like composing music and writing songs. I also have awards for my volunteer achievement. I won the Community Spirit Award at Brisbane North TAFE for all the work I was doing for my community and for helping other students.

It's taken years but now, finally, major organisations want to come on board and help us at the drop-in centre. I don't get paid but what I'm getting out of this is people give their understanding back to me. I speak at forums. I attend mental health case management meetings and speak up for clients if I think the professionals haven't done the right thing. The 'experts' ask me for my opinion. I have over 70 letters of support but we need more funding. It doesn't cost much to run a drop-in centre that helps people get to know each other—the old, the lonely, addicts, those with depression, war veterans—and it's great. We have fun. We even party on! We run a dinner and dance ball each year for the homeless or for those who are experiencing hardship. I have just started a drop-in centre in Nanango. I'm trying to at least get three drop-in centres running this year and another three in 2018. It will happen because I will make it happen. And it's needed.

My real mum is in an aged care home in Mildura. She's got a bit of dementia. I saw her last year at my sister's funeral. My other sister took her to the viewing of my sister's body and I met with all my family there. We keep in touch through the internet. I was the only one in the family who was stolen because I was white. My sister Kerry said to me that she wished that we grew up together. It was wrong that they split us up. It was wrong that the white police went running after my mum to get the white baby off her. That should never have happened.

I live for my daughter and my son. I hate being different. I wish I could just be normal but I try to make a difference in helping other people and I really want justice. I've got complex post-traumatic stress disorder. The only thing I was taught was how to hate and fight. The ones who are supposed to help me—doctors, social workers—are those who in the past hurt me. I don't trust them. I never will. I'm very angry with them all. When I was a kid, they gave me no reason to trust them. How can we be proud Australians without justice? I just wish that I didn't have to do drugs and drink alcohol to forget. There's a song 'Don't Shoot the Wounded, Some Day You Might Be One'. I think about that.

No one was supposed to be in Wolston Park until they were 21 years of age. When I speak about this, I am seen as a problem. It's been proven that I am not the problem because the Queensland Government said 'sorry'. We were just kids. For years people said it never happened. My adoptive mum knew the truth. Hospitals and institutions are supposed to be reliable and so people thought that it was all in my head.

I do have some good points as a person, even though I live in a mind that is scrambled up and confused. I'm not psychotic but what they did to me back then has had a hell of an impact. When things happen that are not your fault, life is a hard blow. I hate what life's done to me. My life was a stuff up. Now I'm a learning junkie. I want to learn more. When I learn, I understand things. If it wasn't for my kids, the people at the drop-in centre and my learning, I probably would have diced myself up. I hope for healing, for my anger to be taken away and to be normal. I want to forgive. While there is hope, there is life. While there is life, there is hope.

PART 3:
THE WITNESSES

6
Brewing Truth: The Priest

I grew up in Brisbane. My father was of German descent and was a naturalised Australian citizen, as they called them in those days. During the Second World War, there was a day when he didn't come home from work. He'd been picked up and taken to the internment camp in Tatura, Victoria. I was only about four and understood nothing about what was going on, just that I missed my father. I witnessed my mother trying to reverse the injustice that had taken place. Back in those days there was no family support. The family was knocked about by that. We hadn't just lost dad, we'd also lost our breadwinner.

My motivation to become a priest was my being impressed with two priests at our parish—the parish priest and his assistant. The parish priest had supported our family quite strongly when dad was incarcerated and after he came home. After I was ordained I worked for five years in parish work. Then I was appointed to be the archdiocesan chaplain for secondary students to Young Christian Students (YCS). So for the next five years I worked part-time in two parishes and part-time with the students. Then I asked the archbishop to allow me to work with the students on a full-time basis.

Sean, the chaplain of Young Christian Workers, and myself were taking Vatican II seriously. Vatican II tried to bring the church out of its ghetto and said that the church exists to make the world a better place. Vatican II wanted the church to identify the problems of the world, which it called the 'Signs of the Times', and to respond to those concerns of nuclear arms, the arms race—all those big problems—in accordance with the principles of the Gospel. So it was quite revolutionary. Sean and I were doing study on it and we were having a lot of difficulty with our peers. We thought it would be good to live under the one roof and support one another. So, in 1973, we moved into this big house, the Lodge, and used it as a meeting place for young students and workers to talk about their lives and Vatican II. In 1974, we came across the work on liberation theology by Peruvian priest Gustavo Gutiérrez. For Gutiérrez the starting point was 'the other'. If I do not place myself in the world of the other, then I do not understand the Gospel. The Gospel emphasises conversion—to 'convert' is to go from one's own world to the world of the other. To be poor is to be part of a social group of races, cultures, peoples and classes. The poor person is a product of our society, and to come into the world of the poor is to come into the action of history. Gutiérrez concluded that to be a Christian is to come into the world of the poor and to know real conversion. We, as a staff at the Lodge, photocopied relevant chapters discussing them together as part of our work with homeless young people and other social justice activities we were engaged in at the time.

Some of the young people who came to our meetings were from very troubled domestic situations and would wander around the streets at night until things settled down at home. There were no youth refuges around Brisbane and authorities could lock up young people who hadn't committed a criminal offence. Sean and I said to these young people that rather than being on the streets they could ring us up and we would pick them up. They could stay at the Lodge and we would take them home when they thought it was safe. So the Lodge also became an accommodation centre.

The Queensland *Children's Services Act 1965* allowed for children to be incarcerated if they were deemed to be in 'moral danger', 'likely to lapse into a life of vice or crime' or 'uncontrollable'. Hearsay evidence was sufficient in court and so unscrupulous police used the Children's Court to clean up their crime sheets. So the main way to deal with homeless young people was to lock them up. Most homeless young people were running away from violence at home and then many police were also being violent to these young people. On the one hand, Children's Services workers at the time had a fairly impossible caseload. They were very poorly trained and monitored so it was easier for them to send a young person to be locked up at Wilson Youth Hospital for psychiatric assessment than it was to do substantial work with them.

One day Sean got a phone call from an aunt of a girl who had been placed in Wilson saying that her niece wanted to see a Catholic priest so Sean went and saw the girl and met up with the manager at the time. Sean came home and suggested that we take on the chaplaincy there together, which we began in October 1973. Sean and I would go to Wilson and see young people individually.

We asked them, 'How are you going? How are you handling this place? Have you had any contact with your family?'—just that very important human stuff. Some of them would ask us if we could write a letter to their parents or someone else significant. In Queensland, kids could be locked up at the age of eight and so some of those kids were illiterate. When boys at Wilson turned 15, they were sent to Westbrook but girls at Wilson were kept on there and most of the girls were incest survivors.

Wilson was such a violent place. I saw young people being restrained. Most of the staff were untrained. I heard the staff call the girls 'sluts'. I hate that word. The boys would be called 'savages'. The dehumanising was just awful. In Wilson there was a magistrate who visited once a month but that was just tokenism.

One senior staff member at Wilson who was a trained psychiatric nurse, said to me, 'I will not stand for violence on my shift. If young people are being violent to one another, that has to stop. If staff are being violent to young people, I get them off my shift straight away.' He worked on the boys' side, and when that nurse started his shift I could see the boys breathe a sigh of relief when they saw him.

Sean and I tried to bring about changes in the system as they were being revealed to us. As we were getting to know how Wilson was run, we were voicing our concerns to people in power there. For example, after four weeks in Wilson, an inmate, if they 'behaved themselves', was eligible for weekend leave with their families but there was no leave for those children who came from outside Brisbane or were brought up in an orphanage or didn't have a family. We thought that we could take a couple of children, chosen by management, out on a Saturday or Sunday. Those children who came to the Lodge on the weekend were so pleased to get out of Wilson for a day. We didn't do anything special because we were impoverished ourselves but someone might be baking a cake and they would help and there'd be good conversation while they were cooking or they'd use the trampoline or they'd be invited to go for a drive with a group of us.

It was day out for them from an institution where they could catch their breath. After we started our chaplaincy at Wilson young people who were homeless or in need started turning up on our doorstep at the Lodge.

We knew a couple of social work students from YCS. They wanted to know how to help. Sean and I said that there was very little follow up from the Department of Children's Services once children leave Wilson and so we suggested that they follow up one ex-inmate each from Wilson with our supervision. These social work students did this and the more they got to learn about Wilson, the more they became concerned about it and these young social workers established the Wilson Protest Group.

There was a girl I remember at Wilson, Tammy, who was about 12. She was one of the children that I would talk to. Tammy always seemed to be spaced out and so it was hard to make a connection with her. Then, one day, I was talking to her and everything was hunky dory. We had a good conversation.

I felt that I could be direct with her and so I asked her, 'Tammy, why is it that we are able to speak together so well now, whereas, on the other occasions, we've not been able to?' She said, 'Oh, I haven't taken the pills they gave me.'

In 1974, I got nominated to attend an international students conference in Maastricht, Holland, and I was due for a bit of long service leave and so I was away for three or four months. About two weeks before I was due to go I heard that Tammy had been certified and sent to Wolston Park and locked up in Osler House with the criminally insane. I couldn't believe it! I rang everybody and anybody that I could to try to get this reversed. She had already gone. People said that they would follow it up. Maybe they did. Maybe they didn't. I don't know but I was gone.

When I came back, I found out that Sean had been transferred to Gympie, over two hours drive from Brisbane. It was really a punitive transfer because we had been protesting against the Vietnam War. We were supporting young Catholics in Vietnam who had been tortured. Church leaders saw us as unpatriotic because Australian soldiers were in Vietnam and we were told that we should have been supporting them. The church in Brisbane hadn't woken up to what Vatican II was about and the social justice message in the Gospel.

I was doing the chaplaincy at Wilson by myself, while grieving the loss of Sean and having to run the Lodge as well as doing my work with YCS. There was so much going on that I didn't follow up the matter about Tammy. There was a girl, Mary, who had been in solitary confinement for three weeks at Wilson. I had tried to see her but they wouldn't let me. Then one day, as I was leaving, I saw this man in a suit, waiting to be let out. We started talking. He said, 'I'm a psychiatrist and I come from the community. I have this horrible job of coming in here and assessing children for Wolston Park.' I noticed that he was wringing his hands. I thought, 'You may be wringing your hands, mate, but you're still doing this terrible, flaming job of sending children up there.'

Anyway, Mary ended being sent to Osler House at Wolston Park and so I went to visit her there because I heard that she wasn't getting any visitors. I'd been to Wolston Park before but not to Osler House. I rocked up there. I said to staff that I was a chaplain at Wilson Youth Hospital and that I wanted to visit Mary. They let me see Mary and I said to her, 'You don't know me. You don't have to talk to me if you don't want to. I'm here because I knew that you were in Wilson and I tried to see you there on at least three occasions and they wouldn't let me so I thought I'd come up to say "hello" and see how you are going.' We sat in lounge chairs and she talked non-stop for half an hour and who walked past? Tammy! I nearly died! Oh my god! She had been there for a year. That poor girl was still there!

On another occasion when I was talking to Mary, she started screaming. This adult patient had crept up on her and sunk her teeth into Mary's arm. There were some very disturbed adult women in that place, and the place itself was probably disturbing them a hell of a lot more. I didn't like the atmosphere of Osler House. It was worse than Wilson. I was absolutely appalled that we would send young people there and have them locked up with those who had been judged by the courts to be criminally insane. Wilson was violent and so I also assumed that Osler House was violent. From what I could see, there was no monitoring, no oversight, and no therapeutic or educational programs of any kind.

Then I met a psychologist who worked there. She kept an eye on the young people being sent to Osler House and tried to get them transferred to open wards. So, as a result, the word on the grapevine at Wilson among the teenagers was the way to get out of the system was to do something to pretend that you were mad so that you get certified and sent out to

Osler House at Wolston Park, then get transferred to an open ward and then escape. I thought, 'Yep! Good on ya. Use the system. The system was using and abusing them. They might as well as do it to them.' For those who did have somewhere to go, it meant that they could go home.

Then the Wilson Protest Group started to get good publicity that was critical of the institution. Every time there was an article in the papers there'd be a witch-hunt at Wilson to try to find out who was the source of information to the media. They assumed it was me and so, in January 1976, I was asked to leave Wilson. They stopped the chaplaincy. I was sacked. Those at the Department of Children's Services had the authority to do whatever they wanted.

I used to say, 'Plenty of juveniles. No justice.' Those young people never saw the system work for them. It was always working against them. They were not represented in courts. They had no access to any kind of advocacy. There were some staff who had standards and did their best during their shifts but there was also dreadful stuff going on. The law was being transgressed. The law said you had to be aged eight or older to be sent to Wilson but I saw six and seven year olds there. Little kids! Totally against the law. Every time anything critical about Wilson was said publicly, the minister would say that Wilson was full of murderers, rapists and arsonists. The media loved that. I worked in Wilson for three years. I never met a murderer or a rapist in there. I met two or three arsonists.

After I got turfed out of Wilson, we did a big study of the juvenile justice system—the police, Wilson Youth Hospital, welfare, their relationships with young people, alternatives to that and recommendations. We established the group 'Justice for Juveniles'. We lobbied for years to get Wilson closed down. Wilson was a hopeless place. It wasn't purpose-built. One boy had described it as like living in wheelie bin. I started to give public lectures.

In 1980, Justice for Juveniles put together a proposal and sought funding for the establishment of a Youth Advocacy Centre. My living at the Lodge and listening to the stories of young homeless people, many of whom had been unjustly locked up in Wilson, told me that the suffering these young people had been subjected to was preventable. Young people needed to see that the justice system could work for them not just against them. Skilled social workers were needed to look at the causes of offending, deal with these, and thus prevent the young person from appearing in court again.

During my study leave I came across several youth legal centres overseas. They were of two kinds: centres for legal advice alone, or centres with lawyers and social workers working together. From the research carried out by Justice for Juveniles, we knew that young people in Brisbane needed much more than that—and so we designed a new model consisting of legal advice, social work assistance for communities, an after-hours service to help young people when questioned by police, consultancy and education for professionals and research. We were successful and, in the next year, Brisbane's Youth Advocacy Centre was established. It's still going.

The situation for children now, in theory, we've got covered. We've got children's commissioners at both federal and state levels. We've got health rights people. But you need two things: you need very strong, solid legislation for the children's commission and good health rights legislation. I'm not sure that we've got that. In Queensland, because we don't have an upper house in parliament, we need to enshrine a Bill of human rights, including children's rights, into our legislation. Also, the current Queensland Family and Child Commission needs to be resourced adequately and commissioners need to be strong in their advice and in standing up to government. Often young people are voiceless and powerless and need people to walk with them. Young people are capable of reflection and drawing their own valid conclusions about what could make systems better. So it is important to listen to them, to advocate with and for them, and also to affirm their dignity.

I grieve that young people have been abused by people who profess to be Christian. What they have done is the very antithesis of what they say they are on about. Also, the way that the church has mismanaged this is heinous, and for them to say 'We didn't understand' is an absolute nonsense from a Gospel perspective. What don't they understand about Jesus saying, 'If you scandalise one of these little ones, it'd be better if you had a millstone tied around your neck and cast into the depths of the sea'? That's pretty plain. I don't think that can be interpreted any other way than in its strong, stark meaning. I don't have any sympathy for those in the church who say 'poor us'. And even with the Royal Commission hearings, from where I sit, I don't see that much change has taken place in the church.

I was pleased when I heard that Leneen Forde was chosen to run the 1998 inquiry into Queensland's institutions for children. The Forde Inquiry was a step in the right direction. There had been a couple of previous inquiries.

There had been the Demack Report into Wilson in 1975, but none of the recommendations, as far as I knew, were implemented. But the Forde Inquiry did not deal with child patients at Wolston Park Hospital. That was a big omission and it also was a reprehensible omission on my part because we didn't include that in our report 'Justice for Juveniles'. Those young people in Wolston Park were well and truly 'out of sight, out of mind'. They were truly forgotten. Former child survivors of Wolston Park need to be given a house and a gold card for health services. The education of their children needs to be supported. That's the least we can do.

I was walking to an appointment this morning and while I was waiting at the pedestrian crossing, a van for a brand of alcoholic drink drove past and big letters on the side of it said, 'Brewing Truth'. I thought, 'That's what I try to do—brew truth.'

7

The Penny Dropped: The Psychiatrist

I was in the paediatric training program at the Royal Children's Hospital and in that job there were two things I remember that influenced my decision not to continue with paediatrics and to choose psychiatry instead. I was in the oncology unit for quite a while, treating sick and often dying children. I found that it was something I perhaps wouldn't want to do for the remainder of my professional career if I was a paediatrician. The second thing was that part of the unit in which I was working admitted children who had been subjected to suspected child abuse and neglect—that involved treating those patients in conjunction with a child psychiatrist. I became interested in the psychological and social factors that brought those children into hospital and the mental health as well as physical impact of the abuse and neglect.

In 1979, when I was 25, after I left the children's hospital, I did a relieving term in adult psychiatry in Lowson House, then the in-patient psychiatric unit in the Royal Brisbane Hospital. Walking into that ward was very different. It was different culturally and with different standards than the children's hospital. Lowson House wasn't as well funded. It was very busy. It was common, in those days, to put out stretchers when they'd reached the bed limit in the four wards. You'd have to walk between old folding stretcher beds in the middle of the ward. When those filled up it was common for the registrar who was on call to go to the open wards and discharge patients in the middle of the night to make beds available for new admissions. I'd come on the next morning and find that some of my patients had been discharged during the night, without telling me, to make way for others coming in.

There were locked wards so I had to carry big lumps of keys on my belt. It was crowded. It was a very different place both physically and socially compared with other wards where I'd worked. There were some older teenagers in Lowson House. I felt it was a place where I could do some good. I was busy—there was lots to do and lots of patients. I felt that these people were really suffering. The view, in some parts of medicine, was then and still is that the suffering from mental illness is not the same as that from other illnesses—that people with mental illnesses aren't as deserving as those with other illnesses. I never felt that. I saw the terror in people's eyes when they were hallucinating or the crushing impact of a severe depressive illness. I felt it was a place where we needed good doctors and nurses. I ended up staying in psychiatry.

I had first been to Wolston Park Hospital as a medical student during my psychiatry term. I went back again during my five-year training to become a specialist psychiatrist, which included a minimum rotation of six months in a psychiatric hospital, which I did at Wolston Park. Then I came back to Wolston Park later in my career as a consulting psychiatrist. In my six months there as a psychiatry registrar I had patients in several wards—in the open ward of Lewis House and in the closed male and female wards: Pearce House and Osler House. I also treated teenage patients. The practices were very restrictive. There was very little patient autonomy or attention to patients' rights. It was very institutional, very controlling. It was basically about containment rather than a patient's recovery. Some of the teenage patients were unhappy and would complain about being in the hospital and for others it had become an alternative home for them, which said a lot about the terrible circumstances that they were in before they got admitted to Wolston Park.

Some of the problems those teenagers were having in the community would manifest in behaviour—acting out—which included self-harm and violence. When those things repeatedly occur, it's not very long before someone slaps a mental health label on the person, which then gets them into the mental health system. That system, for better or for worse, is perceived as the place where that sort of behaviour is better contained because there are locked facilities and mental health legislation that can detain people against their will, but self-harm and aggression don't always

7. THE PENNY DROPPED

correlate with the person having a mental illness. There are many other reasons why people do those things. So I think the mental health system was used to provide behavioural control and that still happens. There is pressure from other parts of the health and welfare system to say, 'Look, we can't handle this person. They're too aggressive or they're threatening self-harm. You've got to take them.'

That's been a tension ever since I have worked in the mental health system. When I see a patient I try to work out what has caused the presentation. The behaviour could be due to psycho-social issues in their home, their family, from substance abuse or a range of things. The treatment would be to try to change those environmental factors rather than treat the symptoms caused by those factors. The problem is that the health system doesn't have control over those environmental factors so if the problem is that the person is being victimised in the family with whom they're living—being abused—or whether they're part of a group of individuals who have antisocial behaviour or substance abuse, mental health treatment of the person does not change that. If you discharge them and they go straight back into that environment, then you're putting them back into the situation where the problems arose. But if you admit them to hospital, in the mental health setting, then you're putting them in a situation where they've got a psychiatric label, they're given medications, drugs, and that isn't going to fix the cause of their problems. So you're in a no-win situation.

When I think about the young patients I had when I was a young doctor, there are two that stand out. There was one teenage patient who I treated and one night I was on call and I walked into the ward and I saw the male nurse holding the patient down, trying to force medicine into her throat. The nurse stopped when he saw me but I reported that incident and that nurse was actually charged. I remember going to court to give evidence over what I saw and I remember that staff member not being convicted but being dismissed for a range of other reasons. Over 30 years later, I got an email from that teenage patient, thanking me for trying to help her. Maybe the fact that someone would stand up for her was something that helped her. When I got that email, I was stunned. I kept the email because you don't often get those sort of things. I often don't hear about the good outcomes. The patients that come back are those who are not making it. If I had to guess, at the time I would have thought she wouldn't have made it, but she did. To be honest, I didn't report him just for her. I did it because I was so angry at the male nurse. I just wanted to stick it to him and that's probably not a good reason. Sure I was sticking up for my patient too, but I just couldn't believe that nurses could do those sorts of things.

What I witnessed was probably just the tip of the iceberg. Much worse things than that went on but they didn't happen when the doctors were around. I just happened to be on call and walked onto the ward and just saw what happened by chance. The medicine was something innocuous, which was one reason the nurse got off, I understand. The process, in the hospital, was to report it for internal investigation. So I reported it to the medical superintendent who I guess reported it to the director of nursing who then initiated an investigation, which I understand, led to that nurse being suspended. The reason that the nurse was dismissed was because they had lots of other concerns about him, as I understand it. My concern was just one and it wasn't proven in court but I was happy to go to court and give evidence even though he was not convicted of that particular assault.

That was the only incident I saw and reported. I heard about a few others but I wasn't directly involved in them. As a registrar I wasn't particularly high up in the pecking order. Working there made me think about whether that's the sort of psychiatry I wanted to do and I decided that I would look after the patients that I had responsibility for, while I was there, as best as I could then to get out of there and move on with my career. I felt it was someone else's job to fix the endemic problems. The hospital was being reformed while I was there in the sense that some of the locked wards were being opened. The number of patients per ward was being decreased so it wasn't as crowded. Beds were being closed. Wolston Park was the largest hospital that existed in Australia. It had something like 2,500 beds at one stage. When I was there it had about 1,000 beds and was decreasing. I thought that maybe when they sort all that out, it will get better.

There was another case I remember. There were two very young girls, aged between 10 and 12. I saw them when I was in the children's hospital doing paediatrics. They were admitted to the child abuse unit. They were malnourished. They were thin. They had eczema. They were really distressed young kids. They had a single mother who I remember was a very obese woman who had multiple partners. She wasn't really looking after these kids. She didn't physically abuse them as far as I knew but they were certainly neglected. We called in the child protection team and they came over and there was this big meeting. I was just a junior doctor but

7. THE PENNY DROPPED

I remember being very offended and being indignant about how terrible this situation was and how we had to get these poor kids away from this hopeless mother. Anyway, the kids were taken off the mother and they were put into foster care. I saw the elder of the two girls years later in when I was a psychiatry registrar, when she was maybe about 16.

I remember her coming up to me and saying, 'You don't remember me, do you?' I looked at her and I didn't remember her and she said, 'You did a terrible thing to me. I saw you at the children's hospital and you took me off my mother.' The penny dropped. She said something like, 'No matter how bad it was with my mother, I was never sexually abused. But when they put me into foster care, I was! I blame what happened at the children's hospital for that.'

I felt my guts fall to the floor. I remember thinking how naive I was and how I was part of the decision to take that 'poor' child away from that 'terrible' mother. I was very judgemental without any thought to where that child was going. Was there a better option for that kid? Should we have left her with the mother and poured the resources that were used in the foster care system into the family to try to help there, rather than to think that the simple solution was to put her into care? That stayed with me. I guess it's all a learning experience but that was obviously a wrong call I was part of back then.

So it goes back to the environment and the problems mental health professionals have when they feel powerless to influence the cause of the problems. Seeing a child and getting them out of a bad situation is perhaps not always the right answer, especially taking a child away from their mother. Obviously we think differently about it now but back in late 1970s and early 1980s I was clearly on a steep learning curve.

I grew up in a middle-class part of Brisbane. I went straight out of high school into medical school, straight out of medical school into the Royal Brisbane Hospital. So my perspective of what was acceptable, what was normal and what wasn't was all shaped by my life and experience. I never went to a private school or anything like that but I did go to a middle-class school in the eastern suburbs of Brisbane and so my take on what I saw was from that perspective. Any kid who didn't get fed in the morning or was too thin or hadn't had their eczema treated by a doctor, well that was wrong and that parent was failing and something needed to be done. I was judging them through my lens. That's what happens. Most health professionals are middle class or upper middle class. They judge what they see coming through the door and in the public health system the patients and their families are often from a much less advantaged environment.

The other thing that attracted me to psychiatry was one of those moments when you realise that you totally missed something important about a patient. It was not something I missed about the physical diagnosis; it was missing something psychological. I went into the children's ward where I was working in the morning and there was a baby that had been admitted overnight. The kid was aged about one or two. I remember saying to the very experienced charge nurse, 'Any new admissions, sister?' She said, 'Yes, doctor.' She gave me the cot number and I went down to the child abuse section and this kid was standing on the edge of the cot. I walked up and the kid put his hands up to be picked up. So I picked him up and he hugged me and I turned to the sister and said, 'Oh, isn't he a lovely kid?' She said, 'That child is disturbed.' I looked at the sister and I looked at the kid who was hanging onto me and I was thinking, 'What's wrong? He's a lovely little kid.' She said, 'That child doesn't know you, has never met you before and is hugging you like you're his father.'

The sister was a woman who had worked in children's health for 30 years. The penny dropped again about how naive I was and how an 18-month-old shouldn't actually be reaching out to any stranger who walks past. I had a lot to learn about judging a kid who has been through trauma. So my initial reaction, whether it was to get a poor kid away from a terrible mother, or thinking a kid was lovely because he wanted to hug me, was all about me and my reaction and not about what's wrong with the patient. So those things stayed with me. They made me think that this is much more complicated, but also more interesting, because it's about biological, psychological and social factors, melding them together, understanding what's really going on and why, and how I can help.

It was and still is important to develop a sense of humility about what I can and can't do and not to over-medicalise everything. Not all problems can be solved by medical solutions. One of the things that attracted me to psychiatry was exactly that.

I remember being a first-year resident in the Royal Brisbane in orthopaedics and they'd talk about 'the fractured femur in bed 11' or 'the dislocation of the head of the radius in bed 13'. Even back then I hated that. I'd think, 'Hang on! Come on! There is a person in that bed'. That way of referring to a patient really ground on me. I'd talk to the patient and knew that I had to treat more than just the injury: what about the rest of that person? In psychiatry, I think about more than the diagnosis, especially if I want to be effective. The fact that I can't influence other factors causing the problem is frustrating but I can at least identify them and help the person pursue a non-medical solution or bring in non-medical resources to help. But if you don't see them you can't start to do that.

Ultimately what I learned in my career is that if I can change the system, I could help more patients indirectly than I could ever help seeing them one at a time in clinical practice. If I could make the mental health system better, I would still help patients even if I wasn't their treating doctor.

Regarding those who were institutionalised as children, I'm not a fan of seeing them continuing to be victims. That's disempowering for them. It can be an attributional problem—their problems coping as adults can be all because of 'How I was treated when I was in that institution'. For most, it was bad before they went into the institution. It was bad in there and bad after they got out. The institution was often one bad experience among many. For me it's about saying, 'Despite all of that, you can overcome it, but those who worked in that system need to acknowledge that what we did then made it worse, not better. We didn't help you then as we said we were going to.'

Some were abused. It was heaping more abuse on existing abuse. For others the system was more benign. For a minority in those type of institutions it was actually helpful. However, we know now putting children or adolescents into institutions is not the way to help. A long-term psychiatric hospital is still part of the mental health system but now only for a very small number of adults with severe mental illness for whom living in the community, even with optimum support, would leave them worse off. Long-term psychiatric hospitalisation is not the right place for the mental health needs of children or adolescents.

8

I Had No Way of Processing What Was Going On: The Nurse

I was born in Brisbane in 1962. At the age of 10, I was sent to an all-girls Catholic boarding school in Toowoomba, Queensland. For the last two years of school, all the girls at my school went to a boys' school—a really weird dumping of two busloads of girls into this school for what was called 'co-education'. It was an intimidating environment to learn in but not intimidating to socialise in. On Wednesdays, you could choose from various activities. One of them was to go to the Baillie Henderson psychiatric hospital in Toowoomba. It was interesting that they even offered it to someone as young as 16. I would go there on Wednesdays and they would put me in the ward where there were severely brain damaged children. I was never given any information as to why they were there. I was just there to spend time with them. It sparked an interest in me to learn more about what situations resulted in people being put in such large institutions. There was always something I could be doing for those children and it was something I wanted to learn more about. I decided that when I left school I wanted to learn more about psychiatry.

The only place where you could study to be a psychiatric nurse was Wolston Park Hospital. I wrote to the hospital and was bussed down for an interview in the nursing school when I was in Year 12. I was accepted. I finished Year 12 knowing that I had a job to go to. When I started at the nursing school, on site at Wolston Park Hospital, I found it to be a positive learning experience. The calibre of teaching was quite high.

Some of the teachers were lecturers in psychology and strong advocates for patients. We were given this mandate that hospitals were changing and that we were expected to be on the front line of that change. We were warned that the changes would not always be accepted and that we would be given a hard time. I was rotated between a four-week block in the school and a four-week block on the ward. The nursing school was not all that far from the main hospital, but it felt like 5 million years apart in terms of what was going on in the wards. Over the three-year training we had to spend at least three to four weeks in each ward of the hospital and so I spent time in every ward. McDonald House remains in my memory and I remember the horrors of Noble and Ellerton houses. They were open wards but people were still restrained and tied to chairs.

Ellerton House was a large, geriatric ward with various wings and very few registered nurses. It was run according to a paternalistic view of care—that all the patients needed was to be got out of bed, fed, sat down all day and made sure that they were quiet. Patients were taken outside wearing hospital gowns and sat on a towel on a chair and their arms were tied to the chairs with sheets.

My attempts at undoing those sheets and walking those patients to the toilet were physically stopped by staff, 'These people are OK. Put them back in the chair.' I would use medical reasons, 'They'll end up with bed sores and end up in the medical ward.' The reply would be, 'You don't need to be doing that. What do you know? We've been working here for years.'

Many of the patients had advanced dementia, Alzheimer's or Korsakoff psychosis, and so they didn't speak or they muttered. As a nurse I always assumed that if you spoke to a patient with some level of dignity and respect you may actually be heard or at least felt. I would just continue to practise doing this and doing this and doing this. For that I was given all the shit jobs—literally—attending to people with impacted bowels. I will never forget talking to his man, explaining to him that it would be very uncomfortable. I remember going through the whole thing and telling him that I would ensure his privacy. I remember saying to him, 'Please, please squeeze on my hand if this is hurting you.'

These were the kind of jobs that I was given because I released patients from the restraining sheets and walked them around. This behaviour didn't change. No one spoke to me in the staff room. Those patients had no voice. The way they were fed was revolting. They had food pushed down their throats. They had no say. That place was so abusive. Wolston Park was a traumatic place and so isolated. It's in the same district as the prison. Some of the men who worked there were ex-screws. They employed thugs. A new wave of educated students was threatening to staff at the time. I reported the abuse to my teachers at the nursing school and said that the physical and mental health of patients were suffering because of the treatment by staff. They listened and supported me saying, 'These are the kind of practices that we have been encouraging people to air but with a system like this, there is so little that we can do.' They behaved like their hands were tied but they supported me in what I was saying. They didn't give any indication that they were going back to Ellerton House to address it but I was very young, only 17, and I didn't pursue it. I do know that the Richmond Report, which came out near the end of my training, meant that the bells were ringing for the end of places like Wolston Park. I think that the school of nursing did too little, too late. The Richmond Report triggered all sorts of industrial disputes. Nurses went on strike when there were calls for the end of institutionalisation because they feared that there wouldn't be any more jobs for them.

I remember years later running into a nurse from my class and I mentioned Ellerton House. She said, 'What do you mean Ellerton House? There has never been an Ellerton House!' It distressed me so much that someone my age had actually wiped out Ellerton House from their corporate memory. I went straight to a psychiatrist after that, 'You worked there. Tell me there was a geriatric ward.' He said, 'Yes. It was Ellerton House.' That nurse had never worked anywhere else except Wolston Park. She must have witnessed so much when she was a student and was prepared to forget.

Noble House was another ward at Wolston Park for people with mixed diagnoses. I remember once when we had to arrange the chairs in a theatre-like setting, semi-circles, so that they could watch Princess Di get married on TV. It was a square room. Usually, the chairs were positioned so that everyone sat side-by-side along the wall in these huge rooms. The idea that you could reorganise the chairs, in a theatre style where people could sit and talk to each other led me to suggest, 'Why don't we kind of try and do this a little bit more often?' 'No', was the answer I got, 'It works perfectly well the way it was.' I was just the fucking student nurse. What would I know?

There was a beautiful older patient in Noble House named Mabel who was put in a single room with white walls. She only was ever given a flimsy gown to wear. Every morning when I arrived for my shift, Mabel would have her shit plastered all over herself and the walls. An Ipswich winter could be as cold as –4°C. Noble House had a registered nurse named Jeff whose surname I've forgotten, probably in the interests of my mental health. Jeff's way of waking Mabel up was to bring in the fire hose and spray it all over her and the room. She would huddle in the corner and scream in pain because of the force of the cold water. He would do this repeatedly. I came in one morning much earlier and got Mabel out of bed and I gave her a hot shower and I also ran her a bubble bath. I washed everything out of her hair. Jeff arrived. I said to him, 'You can't do that anymore. I will bath Mabel.' 'That's not going to happen', he replied. I tried another couple of times but Jeff ripped into me, 'You're not interfering with the way I run this ward.'

I was close to registration and so, on one occasion, they gave me the keys to the drug room to get something for a patient. I opened the door and saw Jeff raping a patient who was in her seventies. I left the door open and stood there and he stopped. I took the woman away. The next morning, I reported him to the nursing school. The following day all my tyres were slashed. I went to the school and said that I needed to be removed from that ward. They agreed that it wasn't safe for me to be there and they moved me.

I also worked in Barrett Centre, which was a whizz-bang new admissions unit for those who required more acute care. Most people were admitted through Barrett A, which was a locked ward. It was a new setting and all about modern psychiatry. It was run by a nurse named Larry. He did things that charge nurses should do, which was hold a staff meeting every morning and allocate patients to nurses, instruct us to write up notes after every session and speak to our patients' doctors, make sure we spent time every day speaking to patients to see how they're travelling, and so on. It was not an easy place to work because it was a closed ward with acutely psychotic people. No one could be in bed after seven o'clock in the morning. I never understood this. Everyone has to be up at seven and out at breakfast and then the bedrooms get shut off. Social workers, physiotherapists and occupational therapists would spend time there and so there was a lot more external transparency.

I came in one day to find a five-year-old sitting in the library. He was hurling books at the window. Then he went for the furniture. He just wanted to get out of the place. I tried to sit with him but he was very angry. His notes were off limits so I couldn't read about his case. All I thought was, 'What the hell is a five-year-old doing in a ward like this with all of these adults?!' He didn't stay there very long and so it must have been a holding place for him, but the fact he was there made my eyes boggle. There was something really, very wrong. It shouldn't have happened.

I finished my training, became a registered nurse and worked at the Barrett Centre. Even though it was more modern there, I felt the need to get away from Wolston Park altogether. It was a creepy place. It was full of creepy people. I worked with someone in the Barrett Centre who had a masters in philosophy and had developed schizophrenia. He recovered and was doing psychiatric nursing. He was a very interesting person to work with and I remember him very well. I remember one night there was an incident during our night rounds. We pointed our torches up to the ceiling or onto the floor, not in patients' faces, so we could see that patients were OK. We found someone who had managed to cut their throat. We called emergency and a whole team of people arrived and rushed them to the Royal Brisbane Hospital. That person died. The mounting trauma was enough for me to think about how I could work in psychiatry elsewhere. I was out of there. Once I registered as a nurse, I got out of Wolston Park as fast as I could.

My role now, at a not-for-profit, is to liaise with people who have been sexually abused and the Royal Commission. I write submissions and I run forums for these people. I think the avenue of there being a public hearing for former child patients of Wolston Park at the Royal Commission has been closed off. They've repeatedly said 'no'. I think the Royal Commission tried hard to engage with these women and to work hard for a public hearing. This didn't happen and now it's just too hard for them. They probably assume that there aren't enough witnesses for a public case study on Wolston Park. If there was a bigger group of survivors, then I think it would be more on their radar.

I think the survivors are right when they say, 'There's a small group of us. They're waiting for us to die off.' The answer from the Royal Commission was, 'We are not doing any more historical case studies.' But the fact is, every case study is historical. It is really about the commission's view of the reliability of witnesses. Also, the Queensland Government has got off so lightly in the couple of case studies that have been done on institutions in Queensland. Instead, there's this focus on elite boys schools, when they should be showing that abuse happens to children from a range of class backgrounds. There's a lost opportunity for the commissioners to recognise and understand someone with a different upbringing. Also it's a 4:2 ratio of commissioners—four men and two women. Because the statistics show one in four girls and one in six boys are sexually abused, I think that there is room to question the 'maleness' of the Royal Commission and its elitism. Yes, they've proven that child sexual abuse is still happening today, but that is not an excuse to not go back and look at historical cases.

The former child patients from Wolston Park received an apology from the state government. That is something that we can go back to and use as leverage. We're hoping that the government has good intentions to take this further. This group of people deserves this redress.

My work connected with the Royal Commission has helped me focus on my experience at Wolston Park. I was working at Wolston Park at a time that coincided with the end of the institution in terms of the idea of asylum. Seeking asylum is something that can be very positive but it also has negative connotations. Setting up a bucolic world of retreat where people are able to take leave from their lives and be treated worked for a period of history, but only for short time. I was there at a time when institutions systematically failed individuals in many ways—in their treatment, the level of oversight, the lack of independence, the lack of transparency, and the lack of places for people to go to afterwards to recount their experiences and get redress.

The issue of children being placed in Wolston Park hasn't gone away. Children who were under care and protection orders were unjustifiably placed in a situation where they were open to any kind of abuse. There was nothing, nothing about their mental health that was pertinent to their placement. It was all about how you construe 'mad and bad' children. This has happened throughout history, particularly to women and children. Within the model of mental health, they are a particularly vulnerable group within the population.

I also think about my reading Hannah Arendt's work when I studied philosophy and the amount of writing she did on violence. 'The banality of evil' is one of her more famous quotes and it fits so well with those who are perpetrators of all kinds of abuse. Evil occurs, for her, when there is a failure to think, to enact the basic principles of a larger humanity. I think this comes as close as possible to what I witnessed at Wolston Park Hospital—an utter failure to think. People went through their lives not thinking.

Back then, when I was a student nurse, I was pretty out of touch with understanding the cause and effect on me personally. I was so young. I had no way of processing what was going on. I didn't know what the word 'advocate' meant. I'd gone from a boarding school to another institution. Former colleagues say to me, 'You were far too young to be in that kind of environment. That was too much to be exposed to for a person of your age.' I say, 'It was too much for anybody.'

PART 4:
NEXT STEPS

9

Conclusion: What Followed and What May Yet Proceed

Goodna Girls is a living history. Since the collection of these oral histories, Tammy, as part of the 2017 South Burnett Regional Council Australia Day Awards, was awarded two certificates of achievement for her volunteer work. On 1 January 2017, Rose finally moved into a home of her own, provided by the Housing Authority in Western Australia, where she is able to live with her daughter Karen.

In terms of a wider policy response, in 2016, the acting Queensland mental health commissioner read my opinion piece concerning the plight of children sent to Wolston Park Hospital.[1] Later, she approached the Queensland Government to support a reconciliation process. In an email to me, she explained:

> I brought to the attention of the Government, in mid-2016, the promise to consult with people who as wards of the State may have suffered harm while detained in adult mental health facilities—this is consistent with the 2010 Apology. As a result, the Minister for Health agreed to progress a process to consult with each of the people that fall within the above definition.[2]

Media attention followed. Meanwhile, the women survivors initiated their own meetings with politicians and bureaucrats to ensure that the consultation process would both be expedient and cognisant of their needs and associated sensitivities. This quest for justice has indeed been

---

1 Chynoweth, 'Who Is Protected'.
2 Email to author, 6 January 2017.

survivor driven. In October 2017, Queensland ministers Cameron Dick and Shannon Fentiman wrote to those survivors who had participated in the reconciliation process informing them of the details of a reconciliation plan:

> We will provide an ex gratia payment … in acknowledgement of the wrong that was done to you as a result of the State's decision to place, you, as a child, in an adult mental health facility.
>
> This payment is not intended as compensation. The acceptance of this payment will not stop you from pursuing your common law rights, and therefore we will not ask you to sign a deed of release as a condition of payment.
>
> We understand that some of the other people participating in the reconciliation plan may not want the amount of the ex gratia payment to be known publicly. For this reason we ask that you keep the amount of ex gratia payment confidential.[3]

The letter also noted the Queensland Government's offer to make additional payments of $1,000 for legal advice, $1,000 for financial advice and $2,000 for professional counselling/debriefing sessions. The government promised to identify an organisation or individual to assist survivors with access to government services; provide information on the impact of the antipsychotics, sedatives and anti-anxiety medications they received as children; and provide access to their health records (until the age of 21 years). The government also informed survivors that the Queensland Police Service would only take action in response to testimonies of criminal and potentially corrupt behaviour if survivors made a formal complaint.

Financial redress had been granted 21 years after a group of former child inmates had met through an invitation to connect, made in Ken Blanch's 1996 article in the Brisbane *Sunday Mail*. Six women from this collective did not live to see this outcome of their years of activism. The significant delay on the part of the Queensland Government to a resolution for former child inmates of Wolston Park Hospital is not the only criticism. The public notification of the reconciliation process was also too narrow. 'Connie', a former state ward who had been placed in Wolston Park Hospital as a child, had only learned of the reconciliation process when it was over. Connie contacted me after the reconciliation process. She wrote:

---

3   Dick and Fentiman, letter to participants of reconciliation process, 17 October 2017.

9. CONCLUSION

> If I wasn't placed on the Government's reconciliation list, and I was definitely placed in Goodna, then how many other girls are there? I never saw any advertisement about it. Not everybody reads the *Australian*. There may be other women that the Queensland Government has not taken responsibility for.[4]

Connie, as a child, was a victim of domestic abuse and incarcerated in Winlaton Youth Training Centre in Melbourne after she was charged with 'neglect'. Then, after having been taken by her abusive father to Brisbane, she was placed in Karrala House and subsequently transferred to a locked ward in Wolston Park Hospital:

> I'd become a sort of nobody-wants-you thing. They drove me mad by putting me in isolation at Karrala and I came out of there in a rage and because of that, they put me in an adult institution for insane people. I was first put into a locked ward in Goodna where I was kept in a straightjacket. Every time I cried I was given a needle of Paraldehyde. I was given enemas. Eventually I was put in an open ward. I was released from Goodna when I turned 18.
>
> I don't want to have to fight for money. I'm on a pension, paying a mortgage and barely surviving. The main thing I want is recognition, not just for me but also for all the women who went through that hell hole. Nothing can compensate for what they did. Nothing. I'm not a nut case but I have depression. I can't get rid of the nightmares. I can't get rid of the daytime flashbacks. I live with it always. I'm 67 years old and I'm still living with it. Why shouldn't we speak up?[5]

Connie attempted to draw public attention to this living history through writing her own autobiography, which has since been published. She was also interviewed on television. She observed:

> The Forde Inquiry was well-advertised. I was living in Western Australia, I heard about it and I put in my submission. The Government didn't look through the records properly as part of the reconciliation process. They also had my name on record because I sent in a submission for the Forde Inquiry. They obviously don't want to know how many women went through hell![6]

---

4 'Connie', conversation with author, 19 December, 2017.
5 'Connie', conversation with author, 19 December, 2017.
6 'Connie', conversation with author, 19 December, 2017.

Connie's frustration suggests that the research conducted by the Queensland Department of Health in preparation for the reconciliation process lacked rigour or, perhaps, that the government may have purposefully restricted the process to limit the numbers of survivor participants.

Do redress payments denote a sufficient conclusion to this living history? The narratives of the women in this book address the violation of children's rights as well as a suite of crimes committed against children. The reconciliation process was conducted in private but is there also a need for a public hearing? John Murray is a Forgotten Australian who, as a child, experienced 11 years in out-of-home care and became a criminal justice activist and political adviser for three members of state parliament. He was the co-ordinator of the Positive Justice Centre, which campaigned for the rights of young people in institutionalised care. Murray was awarded a Human Rights Award by the Australian Human Rights Commission in 2004. He spoke to me about the reconciliation process administered by the Queensland Department of Health:

> There is an assumption that without having a full and frank discussion and understanding of what took place that somehow there will be remarkable change. In addition, the Department of Health—the very same agency that is responsible for the problem is then tasked by the state to respond. That's quite inappropriate. The issue was 'power' then and it's about 'power' now. Instead of sending in another agency, that can have some semblance of independence, the response has to come from the organisation that did the damage. It takes away good faith and takes away power from the victims by recreating the original relationship when these survivors were children. Governments have agencies for these purposes. With just a letter of authority from the minister, they could have used the ombudsman, the privacy commissioner, the attorney general or the law reform commission. There should be an independent judicial review with appropriate processes and experience in dealing with legal and moral concerns—gathering of evidence, taking witness statements, understanding appropriate remedies and writing a report. The only role for the Department of Health is to be an honest participant but not to lead this because they themselves have something to learn. Expediency is attractive and desirable but an independent review could still be quick.[7]

---

7   John Murray, conversation with author, 23 April, 2017.

Such a judicial review could, in addition to examining behaviours of individual staff, investigate the decisions of politicians and bureaucrats throughout this chapter of Australian punitive welfarism. As Murray wrote in the Positive Justice Centre's submission (2003) to the Senate Inquiry into Children in Institutional Care: 'We should not allow that breach of the social contract to go unpunished, for the results of that abuse have been simply astounding'.[8]

In addition to the lack of public accountability of the decisions made by government bodies that resulted in children being interned in adult psychiatric facilities, the exclusion of this matter from the terms of reference of the Forde Inquiry and the significant delay in reconciling with survivors, there is also an absence of publicly available data. Three of the four former child inmates in this book managed to escape from Wolston Park Hospital. They ran in fear for their lives. What would have happened to these young women had they remained? What of their fellow child inmates left behind? Further research is required to determine the number of children who were placed in Wolston Park Hospital and the corresponding number and dates of discharges or, if applicable, of deaths and associated burial records.

On a broader scale, the current system of out-of-home care for children requires thorough and independent examination, given the research that demonstrates the disadvantaged life prospects for these young people. Providers of the institutionalised 'care' of the women in this book (before they were placed in Wolston Park Hospital) are still being funded to deliver child protection services.[9] Good Shepherd Australia New Zealand (formerly the Sisters of the Good Shepherd) runs Warana School for children with mental health issues.[10] The Uniting Church was formed in Australia in 1977 and is a unification of the Methodist, Presbyterian and Congregational churches.[11] Uniting Care in Queensland, which is part of the Uniting Church, runs foster care, family and youth services.[12]

---

8   Positive Justice Centre, Submission 122, Senate Inquiry into Children in Institutional Care, 31 July 2003, at Parliament of Australia, 'Submissions Received by the Committee as at 17/3/05', accessed 30 March 2020, www.aph.gov.au/Parliamentary_Business/Committees/Senate/Community_Affairs/Completed_inquiries/2004-07/inst_care/submissions/sublist.
9   I am indebted to John Murray for this observation.
10 Good Shepherd Australia New Zealand, 'Young People', accessed 16 February 2020, www.goodshep.org.au/find-a-service/young-people/.
11 Watson, 'Performing Religion', 331.
12 Uniting Care, 'Services and Support', accessed 16 February 2020, www.unitingcareqld.com.au/services-and-support.

The Sisters of Mercy, together with the Christian Brothers and the Sisters of St Joseph have formed MacKillop Family Services, which runs residential homes for children referred through government departments in New South Wales and Victoria. It is time to formally and critically reflect on the cultural values that endure beyond the inquiries into Australia's out-of-home care system for children, enabling a nation's trust and tax dollars to be endowed on charitable organisations and government departments that systematically abused children.

Goodna Girls also has implications for our education system in that these women were denied a formal education. Their internal frustration and external rage, then, is not only a response to their captors, it is also a reaction to a learning potential that was left unfostered as well as symptomatic of a justifiable need to be recognised as worthy. If our education policies and practices are to be equitable, they require an understanding that the signifiers of giftedness in children can be mistaken as identical to the trappings of privilege. It is estimated that only 1–3 per cent of care leavers enrol in higher education in Australia and their completion rates are lower than their non-care peers. The 'Raising Expectations' project aims to develop strategies to encourage care leavers to access higher education and support those already enrolled.[13] There is an opportunity in Australia for higher visibility and take-up of education programs that have been designed in consultation with, and specifically target, those who have experienced out-of-home care.

The events that led to the women in this book being placed in Wolston Park may not be explained solely by the notion of the Stolen Generations that emerged in 1982 as a result of Peter Read's published monograph. His research revealed the practice of attempted cultural genocide as a result of intervening visits by government representatives who took Aboriginal children away from their families.[14] However, Judy and Jean/Erin did not become aware of their Indigeneity until they were well into their adult years. It is fair to assume that government child protection services at the time did not know that they were Aboriginal either and therefore their Aboriginality was not the direct cause of their being taken into care. Tammy's transition to Wolston Park occurred during the time that she lived with her adoptive non-Indigenous mother, and Rose is non-Indigenous. These observations do not necessitate a revision of Peter

---

13 Wilson, Harvey and Mendes, 'Changing Lives', 575–76.
14 Read, 'The Stolen Generations'.

Read's thesis. Instead, it is important to additionally acknowledge the wider policies and legislative instruments that enable both Indigenous and non-Indigenous children to be placed in out-of-home care. This, in turn, should inform relevant and inclusive policy responses in the areas of law, social services and education as well as meaningful and inclusive representation in public history.

On 20 October 2016, Judy and Jean/Erin, as part of their determined quest for redress, met with Shannon Fentiman, Minister for Communities in the Queensland Government. Erin spoke about her childhood experience in solitary confinement—the rape, the torture, the neglect and the punitive medical treatment. She has since been offered an ex gratia payment as part of the reconciliation process. Her words still resound as a cry for the end of punitive responses to vulnerable people:

> You have inherited righting the wrongs of the past that both sides of government knew about and were complicit in.
>
> It is cruel what happened to us but it is also cruel what is being done to us now by making us fight for so long.
>
> It is time to finish it.[15]

---

15   Jean/Erin, email to author, 18 June 2017.

Glossary

This glossary provides further information on the institutions, organisations, and government and non-for-profit initiatives, as well as psychiatric medications, that are mentioned in the book.

Institutions

Boggo Road

H. M. Prison Brisbane opened in July 1883 for male inmates. A prison for women was opened on site in 1903. A new female division was opened in 1982. In 1988, the final report of the Commission of Review into Corrective Services in Queensland (the 'Kennedy Report') stated: 'Boggo Road Gaol is a relic of the last century and is hopelessly inadequate to provide corrective services today'. A new women's prison was opened in Wacol, Brisbane, in 1999, marking the closure of the female facility at Boggo Road. No. 1 and No. 2 Divisions had closed in 1992 and 1989, respectively.[1]

Diamantina/Warilda

Diamantina Orphanage opened in 1865 at Sandgate, Brisbane, and was named after Lady Diamantina Roma, who was married to Queensland's first governor. In 1910, the institution was relocated to the suburb of Wooloowin. In 1962, it was renamed the Diamantina Receiving Depot

---

1   Inside Boggo Road, 'Boggo Through the Decades', accessed 12 February 2020, www.boggoroadgaol.com.au/2015/10/boggo-through-decades.html.

and Infants' Home. Two years later, it was named the Warilda Children's Home and Warilda Infants' Home. From 1967 to 1989, it became the Warilda Receiving and Assessment Centre.[2]

Kalimna

Kalimna Vocational Centre for Girls, run by the Salvation Army, opened in 1962 on the site of the former Salvation Army Girls' Home, Toowong. Kalimna was one of three denominational homes for 'delinquent' girls in addition to the two Homes run by the Sisters of the Good Shepherd in Wooloowin and Mitchelton. The 1999 *Report of the Commission of Inquiry into Abuse of Children in Queensland Institutions* notes that Kalimna had the capacity to accommodate 30–40 girls and was divided into two sections, one comprising a hostel area with dormitories and the other with three solitary confinement rooms that were called 'POP', presumably an acronym for 'place of punishment'. The Salvation Army, and not the relevant government department, determined the length of incarceration for young female inmates. Kalimna was closed in 1977.[3]

Karrala House

Karrala House was opened in 1963 within the Ipswich Mental Hospital and was administered by Queensland's State Children Department to deal with 'emotionally disturbed' girls and also for 'incorrigible' girls at the three denominational homes: the Good Shepherd Home at Mitchelton; the Sisters of Mercy's Industrial School for Girls at Wooloowin; and the Kalimna Vocational Centre, run by the Salvation Army, in Toowong.[4] The superintendent of Ipswich Mental Hospital, Dr R. A. Atherton, argued that discipline at Karrala should be prison-like so as to act as a deterrent against 'antisocial' behaviour.[5] The disused Female Ward 3 at Ipswich Mental Hospital was refurbished to become Karrala 2, which opened in 1968.[6]

---

2   Find & Connect, 'Diamantina Orphanage (1865–1910)', accessed 12 February 2020, www.findandconnect.gov.au/guide/qld/QE00192.
3   Find & Connect, 'Kalimna Vocational Centre for Girls (1962–1977)', accessed 12 February 2020, www.findandconnect.gov.au/guide/qld/QE00101.
4   Gahan and Kijas, *The Mental Welfare of Children*, 73–74.
5   Queensland Government, *Closed Report*, 1.
6   Queensland Government, *Closed Report*, 2.

There were public concerns about modes of treatment in Karrala, including long stretches of solitary confinement. Karrala House was closed in 1971 after a new section for girls was opened at Wilson Youth Hospital.[7]

Long Bay

Long Bay prison opened in 1901, in Malabar, Sydney, to female inmates. A men's penitentiary was added in 1914. In 1969, women prisoners were moved to the Mulawa Correctional Centre at Silverwater.[8]

Lowson House

Lowson House opened in the 1930s and was the psychiatric unit of the Brisbane Women's Hospital (and, later, the Royal Brisbane Hospital). Lowson House closed in the 1980s.[9]

Mitchelton

In 1931, the Sisters of the Good Shepherd (later Good Shepherd Australia New Zealand) established the Home of the Good Shepherd, an industrial school in the Brisbane suburb of Mitchelton. School-age girls were forced to work in the Home's commercial laundry. In 1960, it became one of three denominational homes in Brisbane for 'delinquent' girls. In 1966, it was renamed the Mt Maria Re-Education Centre. It closed in 1974.[10] Mitchelton was one of nine convents throughout Australia run by the Sisters of the Good Shepherd, including 'The Pines' in Adelaide, which Senator Andrew Murray likened to a 'prisoner of war camp'.[11]

Parramatta Girls Home

Parramatta Girls Industrial School was opened in 1887, enabled by the New South Wales *Industrial Schools Act 1886*, which underlined the establishment of government-run institutions and the removal, by police, of destitute children found begging or loitering on the streets. It became Parramatta Girls Training Home in 1912, when it was

---

7 Queensland Government, *Closed Report*, 8.
8 McCormack, 'Long Bay Prison'.
9 Find & Connect, 'Royal Brisbane and Women's Hospital (1967–)', accessed 12 February 2020, www.findandconnect.gov.au/ref/qld/biogs/QE00779b.htm#tab5.
10 Queensland Government, *Report of the Commission of Inquiry into Abuse*, 142, 148.
11 Murray, 'Governor-General's Speech', 783.

transferred to the State Children's Relief Department. In 1946, it became known as Parramatta Girls Training School.[12] In July 1973, the Australian Broadcasting Corporation, as part of its current affairs television program *This Day Tonight,* exposed the abuse of inmates at Parramatta Girls Training School, prompting protests. The Minister for Child Welfare in New South Wales announced its closure in April 1974.[13]

Pentridge

H. M. Prison Pentridge was established in 1850 in the Melbourne suburb of Coburg and served as the main high security prison for the state of Victoria. The prison was decommissioned in the 1990s. It has been redeveloped into a complex comprising offices, retail outlets and apartments.[14]

Queen Alexandra

The Queen Alexandra Home for Children opened in 1910 in the Brisbane suburb of Indooroopilly and was run by the Methodist Church (now the Uniting Church in Australia). Within its first year, it was relocated to the suburb of Coorparoo. The Home received children who were state wards. It closed in 1960 and the children were transferred to cottage homes.[15]

Rosemount

Rosemount Hospital, in the Brisbane suburb of Windsor, was originally a residence, built in 1855. It was transformed into a military hospital in World War I and then a repatriation hospital in 1921. In the 1980s, the Rosemount site was used as a psychiatric facility for the Royal Brisbane Hospital. Currently, the Rosemount complex remains part of the Royal Brisbane Hospital and fulfils a number of functions including geriatric rehabilitation, Indigenous health, palliative care and home and community care.[16]

---

12   Find & Connect, 'Parramatta Girls Training School (1946–1974)', accessed 17 May 2015, www.findandconnect.gov.au/ref/nsw/biogs/NE01318b.htm.
13   Chynoweth, 'Rocking the Boat', 302.
14   Wilson, 'Representing Pentridge', 113.
15   Find & Connect, 'Queen Alexandra Home for Children (1910–1960)', accessed 12 February 2020, www.findandconnect.gov.au/guide/qld/QE00146.
16   Queensland Government, 'Rosemount Hospital', accessed 12 February 2020, apps.des.qld.gov.au/heritage-register/detail/?id=602145.

Sandgate Home

Sandgate Maternal and Child Welfare Home functioned from 1944 to 1983 as a convalescent and emergency care home for children whose mothers were seriously ill.[17]

Tufnell

Tufnell Home formally opened on 6 February 1901 in the Brisbane suburb of Nundah and accommodated both boys and girls. Tufnell was run by the Society of the Sacred Advent, an Anglican religious order founded in 1892 in Brisbane by Caroline Grace Millicent Short. The society established schools and children's Homes throughout Queensland. Tufnell closed in 1993.[18] St Aidan's and Margaret's Anglican schools for girls in Brisbane were founded by the society and still operate today.

Waitara

Waitara Foundling Home was established for babies and unmarried mothers in 1898 by the Sisters of Mercy in North Sydney. In 1928, it was renamed Our Lady of Mercy Home. In 1977, it became the Mercy Family Life Centre and provided counselling, emergency accommodation and family services. In 1994, it became the Mercy Family Centre.[19]

Westbrook

Westbrook was a reformatory for boys that opened in 1900 and operated for 90 years. It was named after the district outside Toowoomba, in which it was established, in the Darling Downs region of Southern Queensland. Westbrook became notorious for the abuse of the young male inmates.[20]

---

17   Find & Connect, 'Sandgate Maternal and Child Welfare Home (1944–1983)', accessed 12 February 2020, www.findandconnect.gov.au/ref/qld/biogs/QE01049b.htm.
18   Find & Connect, 'Tufnell Home (1901–1993)', accessed 12 February 2020, www.findand connect.gov.au/guide/qld/QE00172; The Australian Women's Register, 'Society of the Sacred Advent (1892–)', accessed 16 February 2020, www.womenaustralia.info/biogs/AWE4159b.htm.
19   Find & Connect, 'Waitara Foundling Home (1898–1927)', accessed 12 February 2020, www.find andconnect.gov.au/guide/nsw/NE00183.
20   Stathis, 'An historical account of Youth Detention Centres in South East Queensland and their relationship to adolescent forensic psychiatry', 589.

Wilson Youth Hospital

Wilson Youth Hospital was opened in 1961 and accommodated boys up to the age of 14. In 1971, it expanded to take girls up to the age of 17. Wilson Youth Hospital applied a medical model to the treatment of 'juvenile delinquency'; as it was a locked detention facility, it also provided a punitive response.[21] Most of the children sent to Wilson were under care and control orders and were also under the guardianship of the Department of Children's Services; most girls and some boys at Wilson were status offenders (e.g. truancy, underage drinking and underage sex) and had not committed a criminal offence.[22] In 1983, following adverse public attention initiated by the Wilson Protest Group, the Department of Children's Services changed its function solely to a correction facility, and renamed it the Sir Leslie Wilson Youth Centre.[23] A government review, which began in 1993, recommended that the centre be decommissioned.[24] The Forde Inquiry also recommended closure and that it should take place before the end of 2000. The centre was closed in 2001.[25]

Wolston Park/Goodna

'Goodna', an adult psychiatric facility, was founded in 1865 as Woogaroo Lunatic Asylum. Later, it was named Goodna Hospital for the Insane, then Mental Hospital Goodna, then Brisbane Special Hospital, then Wolston Park Hospital and currently it is the Park Centre for Mental Health.[26]

Wooloowin

Wooloowin State Children's Home was the alternative name for Diamantina Receiving Depot and Infants' Home.[27]

---

21   Gahan and Kijas, *The Mental Welfare of Children*, 11, 64.
22   Queensland Government, *Report of the Commission of Inquiry into Abuse*, 121.
23   Gahan and Kijas, *The Mental Welfare of Children*, 64.
24   Minister for Family Services and Aboriginal and Islander Affairs, 'Ministerial Statement', 741.
25   Queensland Government, *Report, of the Commission of Inquiry into Abuse,* 236; Stathis, 'An Historical Account', 595.
26   Besley and Finnane, 'Remembering Goodna', 117.
27   Find & Connect, 'Diamantina Orphanage (1865–1910)', accessed 12 February 2020, www.findandconnect.gov.au/guide/qld/QE00192.

Education

TAFE

Technical and further education (TAFE) institutes are the largest providers of post-secondary education in Australia, and are administered by state and territory authorities. There are 84 TAFE institutes in Australia, which operate over 300 campuses. TAFE offers a wide range of courses that range in length from a few hours to three years, with a variety of attendance patterns.[28] TAFE provides the vocational education and training needs of industry as well as fulfilling the special needs to disadvantaged groups.[29]

Formal Responses

Demack Report

In 1974, the Queensland Government commissioned an inquiry into the needs of youth in Queensland, chaired by Justice Alan George Demack. The commission's findings, published in 1975, are known as the Demack Report. The report recommended the employment of Aboriginal people to assess Aboriginal children before they were placed in institutions or foster care, and that residential training centres be designed to accommodate children in small, family-sized groups, rather than large dormitories.[30]

Forde Inquiry

The Forde Inquiry refers to the Commission of Inquiry into the Abuse of Children in Queensland Institutions led by the former governor of Queensland, Leneen Forde AC. The inquiry covered the period from 1911 to 1999 and examined more than 150 orphanages and detention centres. Over 300 people provided information to the commission. The subsequent report (1992) made 42 recommendations concerning changes in legislation, policy and practice for children currently in care

---

28 Goozee, *The Development of TAFE*, 8.
29 Goozee, *The Development of TAFE*, 10.
30 Commission of Inquiry into Youth, *Report and Recommendations*, 32–33.

or detention, as well as the provision of assistance to former residents of institutions who suffer from disadvantage as a result of their childhood experiences.[31]

Forgotten Australians

Forgotten Australians is the title of the 2004 report by the Australian Senate's Community Affairs References Committee. The report was the outcome of the Inquiry into Children in Institutional Care, the third in a trilogy of reports. The first was *Bringing Them Home* (1997) by the Human Rights and Equal Opportunity Commission concerning the removal of Aboriginal and Torres Strait Islander children. The second was *Lost Innocents* (2001) by the Senate's Community Affairs References Committee about Child Migrants.

The *Forgotten Australians* report estimated that over 500,000 children in the twentieth century experienced life in an orphanage, other institution or in foster care. The majority—88 per cent—of children who experienced out-of-home care were non-Indigenous, domestic Australian children. These are known as the 'Forgotten Australians' and are sometimes also referred to as 'Care Leavers'.

Lotus Place

The Esther Centre, which had been established in 1998, was renamed Lotus Place in 2006. Lotus Place supports those who have experienced sexual, physical and emotional abuse in government and church-run institutions.[32] The Historical Abuse Network (HAN), which was formed in 2000, operates out of Lotus Place. HAN played a leading role in advocating for the Forde Inquiry's recommendations to be implemented, including the establishment of a place that would support victims of institutionalised child abuse.[33]

---

31 The Forde Foundation, 'The Forde Inquiry', accessed 12 February 2020, fordefoundation.org.au/resources/the-forde-inquiry/.
32 Lotus Place, 'Home', accessed 18 February 2020, www.lotusplace.org.au/.
33 Lotus Place, 'Historical Abuse Network', accessed 12 February 2020, www.lotusplace.org.au/getting-involved/historical-abuse-network.

Redress

Redress refers to the process entered into between government and/or religious organisations and survivors to restore the harm done from abuse. In Australia, the states of Western Australia, Queensland and Tasmania offered ex gratia payments for victims who suffered abuse in out-of-home care. The terms of redress under the Queensland scheme did not include compensation for those who, as children, were sent to adult mental health facilities. South Australia enabled Forgotten Australians who had suffered sexual abuse to make claims under its Victims of Crime Compensation scheme. The Royal Commission into Institutionalised Responses to Child Sexual Abuse recommended redress for survivors, comprising direct personal responses, counselling and psychological care, and monetary payments up to $200,000.[34] In November 2016, the Australian Government announced an opt-in redress scheme, inviting states, territories and other non-government institutions to deliver redress to survivors of child sexual abuse.[35]

Richmond Report

The Richmond Report is the 1983 Report of the Inquiry into Health Services for the Psychiatrically Ill and Developmentally Disabled, conducted by David Richmond AO, initiated by the New South Wales Government. It recommended changes to the dominant hospital-based model of care as well as changes to employment to reform the culture of those providing care.[36]

R U OK?

R U OK? is a non-profit Australian organisation that was co-founded in 2009 by Gavin Larkin, whose father committed suicide in 1995. The organisation aims to help the prevention of suicide by encouraging people to ask others 'Are you OK?', thereby addressing the lack of connection or belonging that people at risk of suicide may experience.[37]

---

34 Royal Commission into Institutional Responses to Child Sexual Abuse, *Redress*.
35 Australian Government, 'Commonwealth Redress Scheme for Survivors of Institutional Child Sexual Abuse', Media Release, accessed 12 February 2020, formerministers.dss.gov.au/17434/commonwealth-redress-scheme-for-survivors-of-institutional-child-sexual-abuse-2/.
36 Department of Health NSW, *Inquiry into Health Services*, 5–13.
37 R U OK?, 'About Us', accessed 12 February 2020, www.ruok.org.au/about-us.

Medication

Artane is a brand of trihexyphenidyl HCl; an antispasmodic drug.[38]

Cogentin is a brand of benztropine used to the treat the side effects of antipsychotic drugs such as chlorpromazine and haloperidol.[39]

Haloperidol is an antipsychotic drug, used to treat schizophrenia and is known by its brand name Serenace.[40]

Largactil is a brand of the antipsychotic drug chlorpromazine. In 1965, medical advertisements in the *British Journal of Psychiatry* described the drug as 'psychocorrective'.[41]

Lithium is a drug used to treat manic episodes or bipolar disorder.[42]

Melleril was introduced in 1960 as a brand of the antipsychotic drug thioridazine used to treat schizophrenia. A study in Queensland in 1972 found that patients who were administered dosages greater than the recommended maximum reported vision impairment.[43]

Modecate is a brand of fluphenazine administered by an injection; it is used to treat psychosis.[44]

Paraldehyde is a drug designed to treat convulsive disorders, 'restlessness' and insomnia. In 1940, a New York medical practitioner wrote about his experiment with administering the drug intravenously instead of the standard dose by the rectum, noting the longer-lasting effect of the drug.[45]

'Phenobarb' is a colloquial term for Phenobarbital, a tranquillising drug used to treat insomnia and anxiety.[46]

Serepax is the brand name for oxazepam, a benzodiazepine, used to treat anxiety.

Stelazine is a brand of the drug trifluoperazine dihydrochloride, which was trialled in 1957 on patients diagnosed with schizophrenia.[47]

---

38 Labbate et al., 'Handbook of Psychiatric', 37.
39 Labbate et al., 'Handbook of Psychiatric', 39.
40 Moncrieff, 'Magic Bullets', 39.
41 Moncrieff, 'Magic Bullets', 38.
42 Labbate et al., 'Handbook of Psychiatric', 117.
43 Cameron, Lawrence and Olrich, 'Thioridazine'.
44 Labbate et al., 'Handbook of Psychiatric', 25.
45 Wechsler, 'Intravenous Control', 2198.
46 Uhlenhuth et al., 'The Symptomatic Relief', 905.
47 Macdonald, 'Trifluoperazine Dihydrochloride'.

Bibliography

Baidawi, Susan and Rosemary Sheehan. 'Crossover Kids: Offending by Child Protection-Involved Youth'. *Trends and Issues in Crime and Criminal Justice*, no. 582 (December 2020): 1–23. Accessed 16 February 2020, aic.gov.au/publications/tandi/tandi582.

Berryman, Phillip. *Liberation Theology: Essential Facts about the Revolutionary Movement in Latin America and Beyond*. Philadelphia: Temple University Press, 1987.

Besley, Joanna and Mark Finnane. 'Remembering Goodna: Stories from a Queensland Mental Hospital'. In *Exhibiting Madness in Museums: Remembering Madness through Collection and Display*, edited by Catharine Coleborne and Dolly MacKinnon, 116–36. London: Routledge, 2011. doi.org/10.2307/2621520.

Bessant, Judith. 'Described, Measured and Labelled: Eugenics, Youth Policy and Moral Panic in Victoria in the 1950s'. *Journal of Australian Studies* 15, no. 31 (1991): 8–28. doi.org/10.1080/14443059109387071.

Cameron, M. E., J. M. Lawrence and J. G. Olrich. 'Thioridazine (Melleril) Retinopathy'. *British Journal of Ophthalmology* 56 (1972): 131–34. doi.org/10.1136/bjo.56.2.131.

Carrington, Kerry with Margaret Pereira. *Offending Youth: Sex, Crime and Justice*. Leichhardt: The Federation Press, 2009.

Chynoweth, Adele. 'Rocking the Boat: The Hay Gaol Museum and the Disruptive Narratives of Forgotten Australians'. In *The Palgrave Handbook of Prison Tourism*, edited by Jacqueline Z. Wilson, Sarah Hodgkinson, Justin Piché, Kevin Walby, 295–318. London: Palgrave Macmillan, 2017. doi.org/10.1057/978-1-137-56135-0.

Chynoweth, Adele. 'Who Is Protected by the Royal Commission's Private Hearings? The Case of Wolston Park Hospital Survivors'. *Online Opinion*, 22 March 2016. Accessed 5 October 2019, www.onlineopinion.com.au/view.asp?article=18116.

Clark, Robin. 'Child Protection and Social Work'. In *In the Shadow of the Law: The Legal Context of Social Work Practice*, edited by Phillip A. Swain, 8–21. Leichhardt: The Federation Press, 1995.

Cole, Christine Anne. 'Stolen Babies—Broken Hearts: Forced Adoption in Australia 1881–1987'. PhD thesis, University of Western Sydney, 2013.

Commission of Inquiry into Youth. *Report and Recommendations of the Commission of Inquiry into the Nature and Extent of the Problems Confronting Youth in Queensland*. Brisbane: Parliament of Queensland, 1975.

Commonwealth of Australia. *Royal Commission Act 1902*. Accessed 30 March 2020, www.legislation.gov.au/Details/C2016C00603/Controls/.

Department of Health NSW. *Inquiry into Health Services for the Psychiatrically Ill and Developmentally Disabled*. Sydney: State Health Publication.

Donnelly, Jack. 'Cultural Relativism and Universal Human Rights'. *Human Rights Quarterly* 6, no. 4 (1984): 400–19. doi.org/10.2307/762182.

Education and Training Committee. *Inquiry into the Education of Gifted and Talented Students*. Melbourne: Parliament of Victoria. 2012.

Ferguson, Harry. *Protecting Children in Time: Child Abuse, Child Protection, and the Consequences of Modernity*. Basingstoke: Palgrave Macmillan, 2004.

Finnane, Mark. 'Wolston Park Hospital, 1865–2001: A Retrospect'. *Queensland Review* 15, no. 2 (2008): 39–58. doi.org/10.1017/s1321816600004761.

Gahan, Kate and Johanna Kijas. *The Mental Welfare of Children: A History of Child and Adolescent Mental Health Services in Queensland*. St Lucia: University of Queensland Press, 2014.

Garton, Stephen. 'Sound Minds and Healthy Bodies: Re-considering Eugenics in Australia, 1914–1940'. *Australian Historical Studies* 26, no. 103 (1994): 163–81. doi.org/10.1080/10314619408595958.

Goodall, Jane and Christopher Lee. 'Introduction'. In *Trauma and Public Memory*, edited by Jane Goodall and Christopher Lee, 1–18. New York: Palgrave Macmillan, 2015. doi.org/10.1057/9781137406804.

Goozee, Gillian. *The Development of TAFE in Australia*. Leabrook: National Centre for Vocational Education Research Ltd, 2001.

Howard League for Penal Reform. *Ending the Criminalisation of Children in Residential Care*. Accessed 16 February 2020, howardleague.org/wp-content/uploads/2017/07/Ending-the-criminalisation-of-children-in-residential-care-Briefing-one.pdf.

Human Rights and Equal Opportunity Commission. *Bringing Them Home: Report of the National Inquiry into the Separation of Aboriginal and Torres Strait Islander Children from Their Families*. Sydney: Human Rights and Equal Opportunity Commission, 1997.

Iacovino, Livia. 'Rethinking Archival, Ethical and Legal Frameworks for Records of Indigenous Australian Communities: A Participant Relationship Model of Rights and Responsibilities'. *Archival Science* 10 (2010): 353–72. doi.org/10.1007/s10502-010-9120-3.

Kociumbas, Jan. *Australian Childhood: A History*. Sydney: Allen & Unwin, 1997.

KPMG and Australian Childhood Foundation. *A Proposed Contained Therapeutic Treatment and Care Service: Final Report*. Melbourne: Department of Health and Human Services, 2016.

Labbate, Lawrence A., Maurizio Fava, Jerrold F. Rosenbaum and George W. Arana, eds. *Handbook of Psychiatric Drug Therapy*. Philadelphia: Lippincott Williams & Wilkins, 2010.

Lang, Sabine. *NGOs, Civil Society, and the Public Sphere*. New York: Cambridge University Press, 2013.

McAra, Lesley and Susan McVie. 'Delivering Justice for Children and Young People: Key Messages from the Edinburgh Study of Youth Transitions and Crime'. In *Justice for Young People: Papers by Winners of the Research Medal 2013*, edited by Anita Dockley, 3–14. London: Howard League for Penal Reform, 2013.

McCormack, Terri. 'Long Bay Prison'. *The Dictionary of Sydney*. Accessed 12 February 2020, dictionaryofsydney.org/entry/long_bay_prison.

MacDonald, Roderick. 'Trifluoperazine Dihydrochloride ("Stelazine") in Paranoid Schizophrenia'. *British Medical Journal*, 28 February 1959, 549–50. doi.org/10.1136/bmj.1.5121.549.

McFarlane, Kath. 'Care-Criminalisation: The Involvement of Children in Out-of-Home Care in the New South Wales Criminal Justice System'. *Australian & New Zealand Journal of Criminology* 51, no. 3 (2018): 412–33. doi.org/10.1177/0004865817723954.

McKemmish, Sue, Jane Bone, Joanne Evans, Frank Golding, Antonina Lewis, Gregory Rolan, Kirsten Thorpe and Jacqueline Wilson. 'Decolonizing Recordkeeping and Archival Praxis in Childhood Out-of-Home Care and Indigenous Archival Collections'. *Archival Science* 20 (2020): 21–49. doi.org/10.1007/s10502-019-09321-z.

MacKenzie, David, Paul Flatau, Adam Steen and Monica Thielking. 'The Cost of Youth Homelessness in Australia'. Research Briefing, 2016. Accessed 1 October 2019, www.csi.edu.au/media/uploads/CYHA_FINAL_REPORT _18April2016_v0dqGpT.pdf.

Minister for Family Services and Aboriginal and Islander Affairs. 'Ministerial Statement, Westbrook Youth Detention Centre Queensland'. *Queensland Legislative Assembly, Hansard,* 12 April 1994, 741.

Moncrieff, Joanna. 'Magic Bullets for Mental Disorders: The Emergence of the Concept of an "Antipsychotic" Drug'. *Journal of the History of the Neurosciences* 22, no. 1 (2013): 30–46. doi.org/10.1080/0964704X.2012.664847.

Moore, Keith. 'Bodgies, Widgies and Moral Panic in Australia 1955–1959'. Paper presented to the Social Change in the 21st Century Conference, Centre for Social Change Research, Queensland University of Technology, 29 October 2004. Accessed 22 September 2019, eprints.qut.edu.au/633/1/moore_keith.pdf.

Murray, Andrew. 'Governor-General's Speech, Address-in-Reply', *Senate: Official Hansard, No. 2, 2008*, Thursday 13 March 2008, 783.

Oppenheimer, Mark. 'Folk Music in the Catholic Mass'. In *Religions of the United States in Practice: Volume II,* edited by Colleen McDannell, 103–11. Princeton: Princeton University Press, 2001. doi.org/10.1515/9780691188133-012.

Penglase, Joanna. *Orphans of the Living: Growing Up in 'Care' in Twentieth-Century Australia*. Fremantle: Fremantle Press, 2009.

Queensland Government. *Reconciliation Plan: For Children Who as Wards of the State Were Placed in Adult Mental Health Facilities*. Brisbane: Queensland Government. 2017.

Queensland Government. *Limitation of Actions (Institutional Child Sexual Abuse) and Other Legislation Amendment Bill 2016*. Accessed 26 March, cabinet.qld.gov.au/documents/2016/Aug/LimitActionBill/Attachments/Bill.PDF.

Queensland Government. *Closed Report of the Commission of Inquiry into Abuse of Children in Queensland Institutions: Karrala*. Brisbane: Queensland Government, 2000.

Queensland Government. *Report of the Commission of Inquiry into Abuse of Children in Queensland Institutions*. Brisbane: Queensland Government, 1999.

Queensland Government. *Report of the Committee on Child Welfare Legislation*. Brisbane: Queensland Government, 1963.

Queensland Government. *Report of the Committee on Youth Problems*. Brisbane: Queensland Government, 1959.

Queensland Government, Department of Health. *Fact Sheet 1 – February 2017*. Brisbane: Queensland Government. 2017.

Queensland Productivity Commission. *Inquiry into Imprisonment and Recidivism*. Accessed 16 February 2020, qpc.blob.core.windows.net/wordpress/2020/01/FINAL-REPORT-Imprisonment-Volume-I-.pdf.

Read, Peter. *The Stolen Generations: the Removal of Aboriginal Children in New South Wales, 1883 to 1969*. Sydney: Government Printer, 1982.

Royal Commission into Institutional Responses to Child Sexual Abuse. *Final Report*. Canberra: Commonwealth of Australia, 2017.

Royal Commission into Institutional Responses to Child Sexual Abuse. *Redress and Civil Litigation Report*. Canberra: Commonwealth of Australia, 2015.

Semmel, Bernard. 'Karl Pearson: Socialist and Darwinist'. *The British Journal of Sociology* 9, no. 2 (1958): 111–25. doi.org/10.2307/587909.

Senate Community Affairs References Committee. *Official Committee Hansard—Reference: Child Migration, 15 March 2001*. Canberra: Commonwealth of Australia, 2001.

Senate Community Affairs References Committee. *Lost Innocents: Righting the Record—Report on Child Migration*. Canberra: Commonwealth of Australia, 2001.

Senate Community Affairs References Committee. *Forgotten Australians: A Report on Australians Who Experienced Institutional or Out-of-Home Care as Children*. Canberra: Commonwealth of Australia, 2004.

Sköld, Johanna. 'Historical Abuse—A Contemporary Issue: Compiling Inquiries into Abuse and Neglect of Children in Out-of-Home Care Worldwide'. *Journal of Scandinavian Studies in Criminology and Crime Prevention* 14, sup 1 (2013): 5–23. doi.org/10.1080/14043858.2013.771907.

Stathis, Stephen. 'An Historical Account of Youth Detention Centres in South East Queensland and Their Relationship to Adolescent Forensic Psychiatry'. *Queensland History Journal* 21, no. 9 (2012): 595.

Stratton, Jon. 'Bodgies and Widgies—Youth Cultures in the 1950s'. *Journal of Australian Studies* 8, no. 15 (1984): 10–24. doi.org/10.1080/14443058409386891.

Swain, Shurlee. *History of Australian Inquiries Reviewing Institutions Providing Care for Children*. Sydney: Royal Commission into Institutional Responses to Child Sexual Abuse, 2014.

Uhlenhuth, E. H., Arthur Canter, John O. Neustadt and Henry E. Payson. 'The Symptomatic Relief of Anxiety with Meprobamate, Phenobarbital and Placebo'. *American Journal of Psychiatry*, (1959): 905–10. doi.org/10.1176/ajp.115.10.905.

Ungsuchaval, Theerapat. 'NGOization of Civil Society as Unintended Consequence? Premises on the Thai Health Promotion Foundation and its Pressures Towards NGOs in Thailand'. Paper presented at 12th International Conference of the International Society for Third Sector Research, Ersta Sköndal University College, Stockholm, Sweden, 28 June – 1 July 2016.

Ward, Lester F. 'Eugenics, Euthenics, and Eudemics'. *The American Journal of Sociology* 18, no. 6 (1913): 737–54.

Watson, Sophie. 'Performing Religion: Migrants, the Church and Belonging in Marrickville, Sydney'. *Culture and Religion: An Interdisciplinary Journal* 10, no. 3 (2009): 317–38. doi.org/10.1080/14755610903287716.

Wechsler, I. S. 'Intravenous Control of Paraldehyde for the Control of Convulsions'. *Journal of the American Medical Association*, 1 June 1940, 2198.

Wilson, Emily. *Prevention is Better than Cure: Eugenics in Queensland 1900–1950*. Melbourne: Australian Scholarly Publishing, 2010.

Wilson, Jacqueline Z., Andrew Harvey and Philip Mendes. 'Changing Lives: Improving Care Leaver Access to Higher Education'. *Oxford Review of Education* 45, no. 4 (2019): 575. doi.org/10.1080/03054985.2019.1596074.

Wilson, Jacqueline Z. and Frank Golding. 'Latent Scrutiny: Personal Archives as Perpetual Mementos of the Official Gaze'. *Archival Science* 16, no. 1 (2016): 93–109. doi.org/10.1007/s10502-015-9255-3.

Wilson, Jacqueline Z. 'Representing Pentridge: The Loss of Narrative Diversity in the Populist Interpretation of a Former Total Institution'. *Australian Historical Studies* 36, no. 125 (2005): 113–33. doi.org/10.1080/10314610508682914.

Winter, Stephen. 'Australia's Ex Gratia Redress'. *Australian Indigenous Law Review* 13, no. 1(2009): 49–61.

Newspapers

ABC News (online)
ABC Radio (online)
The Courier Mail (Brisbane)
Crikey (online)
The Guardian (online)
The Irish Times (online)
The Sunday Mail (Brisbane)

www.ingramcontent.com/pod-product-compliance
Lightning Source LLC
Chambersburg PA
CBHW041313240426
43669CB00024B/2978